PRAISE FOR

BREAKING NEWS:
How to Tell What's REAL from What's RUBBISH

'Newsflash: I loved it.'
Eoin Colfer,
author of *Artemis Fowl*

'A perfect read for any budding
young journalists out there.'
Konnie Huq,
BBC Blue Peter presenter
and author of the *Cookie!* series

'Jam-packed with fascinating
facts, this is a fantastically funny and
much-needed guide to navigating
the news.'
Rashmi Sirdeshpande,
author of *Dosh*

For my parents

First published in Great Britain in 2021 by Simon & Schuster UK Ltd

Copyright © 2021 Nick Sheridan

1 3 5 7 9 10 8 6 4 2

Simon & Schuster UK Ltd
1st Floor, 222 Gray's Inn Road
London WC1X 8HB

www.simonandschuster.co.uk

www.simonandschuster.com.au

www.simonandschuster.co.in

Simon & Schuster Australia, Sydney

Simon & Schuster India, New Delhi

A CIP catalogue record for this book is available from the British Library.

PB ISBN 978-1-3985-0678-7

eBook ISBN 978-1-3985-0679-4

eAudio ISBN 978-1-3985-0680-0

Printed and bound by CPI Group (UK) Ltd,
Croydon, CR0 4YY

MIX
Paper from
responsible sources
FSC® C020471

BREAKING NEWS

HOW TO TELL WHAT'S REAL FROM WHAT'S RUBBISH

NICK SHERIDAN

CONTENTS

TELLING STORIES

INTRODUCTION

Well, hello!

If you've picked up this book, then I'm guessing you're already curious about **the world of news**. Or perhaps you've stumbled across a copy in a bus station. If so, please return it to my publisher, along with the half-eaten egg-and-cress sandwich that I've been using as a bookmark.

I'm Nick Sheridan and I'm a journalist. In fact, you could say that I've been a journalist since the age of eleven when I started my own newspaper, the Daily Font, where I was Editor-in-Chief, Publisher, News Reporter, Sports Correspondent, Weatherman, Columnist, Lawyer, Receptionist, Canteen Chef and Cleaner. Due to funding cuts I was eventually forced to sack every member of staff and finally myself.

Now I'm an actual journalist and I love my job, but let's face it, news can be tricky to navigate. At best it can be interesting, illuminating and uplifting, like the story of the schoolboy who was rescued after falling into an eight-ton lasagne at a local food festival, but more often than not, news can be hard to **understand**, **bewildering** or even a bit **upsetting**.

And then there's **FAKE NEWS**, some of which is funny and entertaining, some the complete opposite. **Fake News** has existed since the dawn of time. Ancient rulers made up rude stories about their enemies, and kings forced painters to make them look more dashing and handsome than they actually were. But in the modern world, we have endless amounts of information at our fingertips. That means there's an even greater risk of falling for Fake News.

As a journalist, it's my job to **cut through the noise** and make sure the truth is heard. So, if you want to take a peek behind the headlines, find out from a real-life journalist how news works, how to **sniff out** the best stories and how to tell the fact from the phoney — then you've picked up the right book.

Breaking News will help you to become a well-informed **super-savvy consumer of information**, satisfy your curiosity about how stories get made, teach you how to write like a journalist . . . and, if you want to follow in my footsteps, show you how to become one!

If that doesn't sound like much fun to you, then this is your last chance to back out. Once you turn this page, it will be too late.

Still here? Good! Let's get going.

Nick Sheridan

NEWS YOU CAN USE

Like any skill — pole-vaulting, pottery,
mimicking the calls of various farmyard animals —
the best thing to do is to learn the basics first.

So it's time to roll up your sleeves and . . .

CHAPTER 1

...READ ALL ABOUT IT!

What is News?

If I was to be a bit of a smarty-pants and try to show off some fancy words, I'd tell you that this is the definition of news (try not to doze off halfway through reading the sentence – as sentences go, it's an extremely boring one):

'The investigation, collation and publication of new events and data to the general public, with the aim of disseminating information for the advancement of a democratic, transparent and informed society.'

THUNK! I actually fell asleep while writing that sentence and whacked my face on the keyboard.

Now that I've managed to get most of the swelling down on my forehead, let me show you a magic trick.

What if I told you that I could delete **all but ONE** word from the definition above and it would still tell you what news is.

Think I can pull it off? **WATCH ME.**

new

Told you I could do it!

No matter how many different words we use to describe what news is, it can be summed up using one simple word: 'new'. It's a story about something that just happened.

It could be the story of me having to plug my nose with tissue paper after I whacked it on my keyboard. That's something that's just happened, which makes it '**new**' and therefore '**news**'.

News is like oxygen, water and sand in your trousers after a long picnic on the beach: you'll find it pretty much everywhere. It comes at us at *lightning speed –*

The news often takes us by surprise, with stories leaping out at us like a jungle puma whose nap has been interrupted. Throughout this book, you'll find **SURPRISE STORIES** – examples of when the news can come out of nowhere and give you a **BONK** on the head. Keep an eye out for Surprise Stories, in this book and in real life.

The news NEVER stops.

It comes at us twenty-four hours a day, seven days a week. Even when we're sleeping, the news machine is wheezing and grinding out top stories. Because something is always happening somewhere. There are always new events to tell the world about.

People who create the news – **reporters, presenters, editors, camerapeople, online writers, technical boffins** etc. – work incredibly hard to get information into our

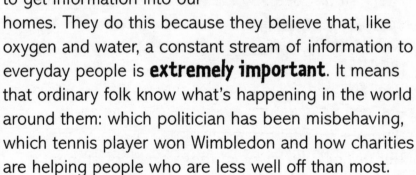

homes. They do this because they believe that, like oxygen and water, a constant stream of information to everyday people is **extremely important**. It means that ordinary folk know what's happening in the world around them: which politician has been misbehaving, which tennis player won Wimbledon and how charities are helping people who are less well off than most.

But it's important to think about how these news stories are made.

Let's say, for example, you're in the school canteen and the person behind the counter hands you a bubbling bowl of **mystery stew**. You're probably going to want to know what ingredients went into the stew before you decide to tuck in.

Discovering what goes into news-making is rather like discovering what went into that mystery stew. Once you know what ingredients are used, then you can decide whether you want to gulp it down or say '**No thanks**' and have something else.

Similarly, if you see a headline or a story that makes you a wee bit anxious, upset or even frightened, finding out more about it will either make you feel better or help you to avoid those types of stories the next time.

That's where this book comes in – to guide you through every aspect of the news.

CHAPTER 2

GOOD NEWS, BAD NEWS

Have a look at this news story and see if you notice anything strange about it:

The
Jolly Good News

Aeroplane lands with no problems whatsoever

A FlyRight plane landed at its destination airport this morning, with no problems whatsoever.

The 11:10 arrival from Paris touched down five minutes early, with passengers applauding the skill of the pilot.

'It was a perfect journey,' said one passenger after landing. 'I had so much legroom, the food was absolutely delicious and the cabin crew were the friendliest people I've ever met.'

'Ten out of ten,' said another passenger. 'I can safely say that that was the best flight I've ever been on.'

All of the passengers disembarked safely and made it to their connecting flights and taxis without a single item of luggage being lost.

'Oh! What a wonderful morning!' shrieked one woman carrying a very well-dressed and well behaved child. 'FlyRight Airlines, how can I ever thank you for such fantastic flight?!'

Have you ever seen an article or a news report about a flight like that? Probably not, because the news tends to report things that are **OUT OF THE ORDINARY**, and a lot of out-of-the-ordinary things that happen are not very nice.

It's normal for these news stories to make you feel sad, angry and even confused. But don't worry, they make adults sad, angry and confused too. It's important to remember that just because we see bad things or bad people on the news, **99.99999999999 per cent** of what goes on in the world happens because of people who are trying to do **good**.

That perfect pilot who flew the plane from Paris isn't going to be on the news tonight. **Why?** Because good pilots and good people make up most of the world. There's nothing 'out of the ordinary' about them. But just because we don't always see them in newspapers or on our TVs, **it doesn't mean they don't exist**.

The stories that **make it** into the news are often about this kind of stuff:

- People who do things that HURT other people or themselves

- People who feel BAD about themselves and ANXIOUS about the world around them

- Traffic ACCIDENTS where people lose their lives

- People who are UNWELL and believe they need to put alcohol or harmful drugs into their bodies to feel better

- People who DON'T have a house to live in

- People who DISLIKE OTHERS because of their skin colour, where they come from, how they look, or who they fall in love with

- VIOLENCE close to home and violence far away, where people fight each other or even go to war over disagreements

- **DANGEROUS JOURNEYS** made by people who escape conflicts in their home countries

- **NATURAL DISASTERS** like tsunamis or forest fires that can mean people lose their homes, or even their lives

- **DISEASES** that make people very sick and sometimes cause death

And lots of other really difficult subjects.

Maybe you've seen something online that you didn't like, or something on TV that made you feel unsafe. When you see stories like that, you might have questions about them. And I'm going to let you in on a little secret when it comes to speaking up or speaking about news:

There is NO SUCH THING as a stupid question.

If you've ever read a story or watched a video that made you feel uncomfortable or sad, here are some of the un-stupid questions you could ask:

WHO ARE THE PEOPLE IN THIS VIDEO?

IS THIS STORY REAL?

AM I IN ANY DANGER?

IS IT OKAY THAT I FEEL UPSET OR FRIGHTENED BY THIS?

WHAT'S HAPPENING IN THIS VIDEO?

When you're deciding who to ask, it's best if you go to someone who you trust – like a **teacher**, a **parent**, whoever **takes care of you**, or an older **friend**. They might not know the answer, but they can try to find out for you. And hey, if you don't feel like asking questions, that's absolutely fine too.

The answers to these questions might make us feel better, or they might not. They might create even more questions. And it's okay to still feel a wee bit anxious if we don't like the answers.

When BAD NEWS gets me

down, here's what I do to cheer myself up:

BAKE some brownies
(and try to not burn the house down)

Drink an ENORMOUS mug of hot chocolate

Go OUTSIDE and run around in the fresh air

Take a REALLY long bath
(three hours and forty minutes is my record)

Watch a FILM that makes me laugh

HUG a friend or family member

Chat to my PALS about what's made me sad

Watch some videos of CATS on the internet

One of these ideas might also help you feel better if
bad news gets too much, but always remember that

there's GOOD NEWS everywhere!

Sometimes you hear news that makes you **smile**. It reminds you that most people in the world are kind, decent and generous.

And telling stories about those people is one of the great parts of being a journalist.

Here are some of my favourites. They're the ones that remind me of the value of stories, especially those with a happy ending.

 A football coach for a kids' team was sad to hear that some families in his neighbourhood couldn't afford to buy new football boots for their kids. He decided to take action and put out an advert for donations of second-hand boots.

It worked! Over 150 pairs of boots were donated, helping kids from less well-off families to keep lacing up and hitting the back of the net.

☺ Poor Max the spaniel lost the use of his back legs when he fell off a bed, but his owner's local community came to the rescue – clubbing together to buy him a doggie wheelchair. Now he's back to **WHIZZING** along the beach.

☺ When coronavirus started spreading around the world, many nursing homes stopped allowing visitors, to keep the folks inside safe. Unfortunately, that meant that many residents felt lonely. But a petting zoo came up with a brilliant solution: they brought some big hairy alpacas to their local nursing home and had an alpaca parade past the windows.

The residents LOVED it!

CHAPTER 3

TALES AS OLD AS TIME

People have been hungry for news since the beginning of time. Picture the very first caveperson telling another caveperson a hilarious story that happened while they were out hunting and gathering ('Zog's bearskin loincloth ripped at the bum LOL.') This is news, even if it's not what we think of as news today.

But the news in those times wasn't much to report on. People cared about where they were going to sleep and what sort of horrific animal was planning on eating them. Or perhaps they were wondering what that big yellow ball in the sky was. But as communities grew and spread out across larger areas, it slowly became more important to know what was happening outside the four walls of one's cave.

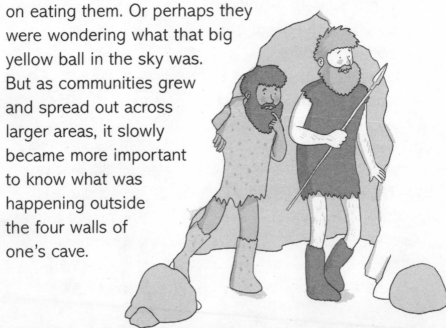

JULIUS CAESAR was a Roman emperor famous for being a great politician and military leader, right up until his pals decided they'd had enough of him and poked him full of holes in 44 BCE. Among the things he's famous for is the 'Acta Diurna', which roughly translates as 'Daily Public Records'.

These were usually carved into metal or heavy stone tablets, but they were basically the **very first newspapers**. They would have been quite difficult to deliver on a paper round, but (I presume) very effective for swatting wasps.

Fortunately there was no need to carry one of these home, as the tablets were stuck up in public places so that the rich folks (the only ones who could read at the time) could catch up on all the events of the previous days and weeks. That meant crimes, trials, marriages, deaths and the birth of important babies (or at least, babies who had important parents).

After a few days, the news that was chiselled into these tablets went out of date and the stones were taken down and replaced with new ones. And with that, **the idea behind newspapers was born**.

Around 100 BCE, powerful families in China had also decided that they needed a way of getting the news. Important events that took place in the palaces of politicians and dynasties were collected and recorded, often on wooden blocks. These became known as '**dibao**' – 'palace reports' or 'imperial bulletins'. Again, these were only read by rich and powerful people, to keep them up to date on all the gossip and events that were happening in the heart of the government.

Both the 'Acta Diurna' and the 'dibao' could be described as the **world's first newspapers**. But they had a very narrow audience.

Then, in the 1400s, something amazing happened that changed the world for ever. In Strasbourg, France, a German guy called **JOHANNES GUTENBERG** invented the **printing press**: a machine that could create lots of copies of articles and books in one go.

First printing press

Suddenly, words were flying all around Europe at top speed. More and more people were learning to read, and they were discovering amazing ideas that had been put down on paper hundreds of miles away.

Soon collections of these stories were being put together and sold to everyday people in Europe, who could read about what was happening all around the world. Sure, it took a while for the story to travel **hundreds or thousands of miles** (weeks and months sometimes), but the news would eventually arrive.

ver the centuries, the printing craze spread from Germany to Italy to the United States, and people began to publish newspapers as we know them today. However, while the writers may have been brilliant journalists, their choice of names left something to be desired. While modern newspapers have flashy and punchy titles, such as the **Star**, the **Times** and the **Record**, early newspapers had much more long-winded names. For example:

Collection of
ALL DISTINGUISHED
and
COMMEMORABLE NEWS

CURRENT EVENTS
FROM ITALY, GERMANY ETC.

The Edwardsville INTELLIGENCER

As decades and centuries rolled on, new inventions made it easier for journalists and printers to make many copies of newspapers. The invention of the rotary printing press in 1843 was a **huge** moment. This machine used huge cylinders to roll the paper through the press. That meant the printer didn't have to start and stop to feed new pages into the machine, making the process of printing papers quicker and more efficient!

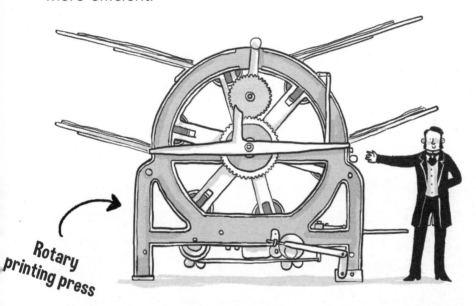

Rotary printing press

But there remained a problem:

MOST PEOPLE COULDN'T READ.

It was only in the 1700s and 1800s that most Europeans started learning to read and write. Arguments between different parts of the Christian faith meant that people wanted to be able to read the Bible for themselves and make up their own minds. It was also a time, known as the **Industrial Revolution**, when machinery was being used more and more by businesses. But to get a job operating the machines you had to be able to read the measurements of what you were making!

Complicated machinery

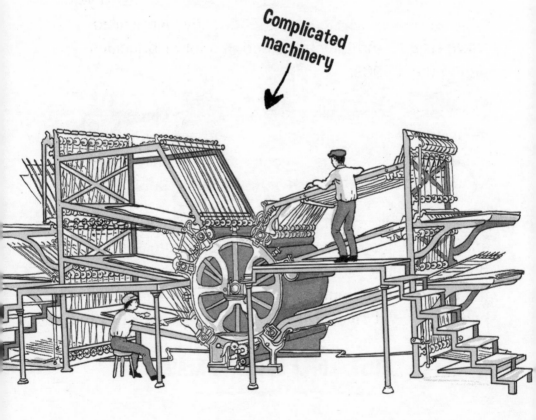

With many ordinary folks unable to read the news for themselves, someone had to do it for them. One of the earliest examples of a newsreader looked very different to the presenters we see on TV today. Instead of sparkling white teeth, a perfect tan and a beautiful tie, these newsreaders wore colourful robes,

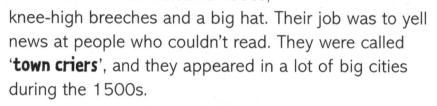

knee-high breeches and a big hat. Their job was to yell news at people who couldn't read. They were called '**town criers**', and they appeared in a lot of big cities during the 1500s.

Town criers would bellow: **'OYEZ, OYEZ!'** which basically means: 'Everyone be quiet because I have something important to say.' Perhaps your teacher should try shouting that the next time your class gets a bit rowdy.

It was the town criers' job to shout news stories and announcements in the street, but they also had other duties. At public hangings, they would read out why the person was about to be executed, and they also had to help **get rid of the body** afterwards, which is the side of the job I wouldn't have fancied doing.

But as the Industrial Revolution paved the way for more people to learn to read, old ways of spreading news died out. In the Wild West of the United States, they had their own version of town criers called '**news men**' who would travel from town to town reading papers to the locals. They were eventually replaced by deliveries of weekly and daily newspapers that people could read themselves.

With the invention of the telegram, the wireless and eventually the television, those public places became private: you could get up to date with the news from the comfort of your front room, your kitchen and now (thanks to smartphones) from **your bed**!

IDA B. WELLS

You might not have heard of Ida B. Wells, but she was one of the most brilliant, butt-kicking journalists of all time.

When she was born, Black people in America were still being treated as objects to be bought and sold. Where she lived, in Mississippi in the United States, many thought that Black people shouldn't have the same rights as white people.

Ida had a very hard early life – both her parents and one of her siblings died of a disease called 'yellow fever'. She got a job at the age of sixteen as a teacher and then began to write articles and columns about how badly Black people were being treated, which would have been very dangerous at the time.

Throughout her life, she wrote and spoke in defence of Black people and also led campaigns to get women the right to vote. She died in 1931 and is remembered as one of the brightest and best journalists America has ever seen.

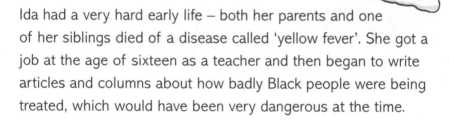

'The people must know before they can act, and there is no educator to compare with the press.'
– **Ida B. Wells**

CHAPTER 4

FAKE, FIB OR PHONEY?

Unfortunately, because there is so much information coming at us every hour of every day, it can be easy to fall for made-up stories.

Sometimes, people make up news as a joke. These are called **spoof** stories, like the one about the pensioner who realised he'd been posting his letters into the dog-poo bin for years! It wasn't true, but it gave plenty of folks a belly-laugh.

Many of these stories are genuinely funny, but most writers will make it clear on their social media account or website that it's entirely made up. They're not looking to fool the reader; they've made up the story so that we can have a giggle.

A lot of **FAKE NEWS** is funny too, but problems start when people believe that Fake News is real.

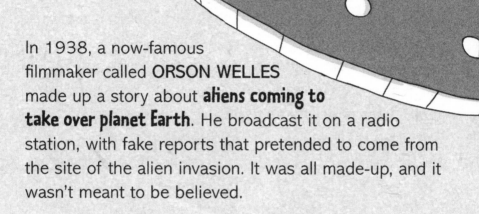

In 1938, a now-famous filmmaker called **ORSON WELLES** made up a story about **aliens coming to take over planet Earth**. He broadcast it on a radio station, with fake reports that pretended to come from the site of the alien invasion. It was all made-up, and it wasn't meant to be believed.

> # But guess what?
> # People BELIEVED it!

Policemen stormed into the studio, demanding that Orson stop broadcasting because listeners were panicking. Hundreds of people were rushing about like headless chickens, packing their bags and trying to flee in their cars and escape these awful monsters. These folks actually believed that aliens were coming to Earth, because they heard it on the radio! Orson Welles apologised afterwards, saying that he had no idea that listeners would think the story was real.

And that wasn't the first time that **FAKE NEWS** was believed to be true. It's been around since the **dawn of time**.

Have you heard of the ancient Greeks? Well, it turns out that around 600 BCE they had their fair share of Fake News. Many ordinary Greeks ate mostly corn, and they were terrified that there would be a shortage. Some tricksy merchants figured out that if they spread fake reports of storms and bad crops then their customers would panic that the corn would soon be in short supply and pay **MASSIVE** amounts of money for any they could get their hands on. The stories about bad crops were untrue, of course, but the corn merchants got very rich as a result!

In 332 BCE, a super-soldier and ruler called **ALEXANDER THE GREAT** (I wish I was called Nick the Great) began to spread the word that he was the son of . . . wait for it . . . Zeus. Yup, the god of thunder and lightning. Dumping the normal-sounding 'Alexander', he started to call himself '**Zeus Ammon**' – which basically means '**Zeus is my dad**'. Lots of people believed in Zeus and his family of gods at the time, so this made Alexander seem almighty.

Two thousand years ago, the Romans were fighting among themselves about who would rule the Roman Empire. One of the contenders for the job, **OCTAVIAN**, began to spread **NASTY RUMOURS** about his opponent, a guy called **MARK ANTONY**.

Octavian wrote and published poems claiming that Mark Antony was drunk all of the time (which he wasn't), and he even had Fake News printed on coins so that lots of people would see it. If there had been social media in those days, he probably would have posted something like this:

OCTAVIAN
@bestemperor

OMG @MarkAntony is such a loser – drunk all the time and his ratings are awful. He would be such a terrible ruler. SAD!

◀ 750 ★ 800

And guess what . . .

the Fake News worked. Octavian eventually won the war.

REBELS
@georgeout

LOL @KingGeorgeII is not looking too good . . . probably gonna croak in a few weeks . . . SAD! ☹

◀ 750 ★ 800

In the 1700s, **KING GEORGE II** of England was also the victim of Fake News. He was ruling over Ireland at the time, but a group of rebels were trying to take back control of the country. The king wanted to be seen as a strong, no-nonsense ruler, so you can imagine how furious he was when the rebels started spreading Fake News about him being ill. They printed the lie in several newspapers and it spread and spread until people began to believe it was true.

In 1835, a US newspaper called the *New York Sun* published a whole series of articles about life on the Moon. The writer claimed that they had seen, first-hand, all the wonderful and weird creatures that live there, including two-legged beavers and unicorns. It was Fake News, but guess what?

People BELIEVED it.

Over the years, the number of newspapers and eventually broadcasters grew dramatically and so too did the amount of Fake News.

One of the most bizarre recent examples of Fake News was in 2019, when climate-change activist **GRETA THUNBERG** was accused of being everything from a time-waster to a **time-traveller**.

A photo taken in the late 1800s of a girl who bears a striking resemblance to Greta appeared in articles in which the so-called 'journalists' insisted she was a supernatural being, instead of a young woman concerned for the world around her. These articles also claimed that her 'character' was being played by an actress, that she had spent time with terrorist organisations and lots of other accusations that turned out to be

**TOTAL.
AND.
ABSOLUTE.
UTTER.
NONSENSE.**

We have to be **VERY careful** when we talk about Fake News, though. In recent years, politicians who don't like what news organisations say about them have started to dismiss the stories as Fake News, even if they're **true**. Calling a true story Fake News means that no one knows what to believe and who to trust. Fake News is definitely a real thing, but just because a politician says something is fake, **that doesn't make it so**.

Although lots of fake information immediately sounds ridiculous, there are other times when it's not as easy to pick up on.

Here are a few tips on how to spot FAKE NEWS

Use your common sense – the little voice inside your brain that says: 'That doesn't sound very likely,' or 'Surely that can't be true?'. If that little voice thinks something isn't right, then you should be extra careful.

Look and see who is posting the information. If the article or video doesn't say who wrote or made it, ask yourself why they don't want you to know. Might it be that what they're saying isn't true?

What emotions is the article or video making you feel? If it's making you sad, angry or even a bit scared, ask yourself why. Is the video meant to make you **ANGRY?** Angry about what? Angry about who?

Sometimes Fake News is spread to make us dislike other people or groups of people. Some Fake News will try to blame a particular person or part of society for problems the world is facing. Ask yourself '**Is that true?**' and '**Is that fair?**'

If a photo or video says it was taken in a certain place at a certain time, use the skills that you'll learn in this book to look for clues. If the person who has posted the photo or video says it was taken this morning, then why does it look old and grainy? If the person who posted it says it was taken in London, then why can you see the Eiffel Tower in the background? Small clues like this can help journalists decide whether news is real or fake.

CHAPTER 5

FAKE NEWS OR REAL REPORTING?

The real world can sometimes be just as strange as the world of Fake News, which makes it even harder to tell true stories from made-up ones.

Here are a few articles that may or may not be real news stories. It's up to you to decide whether you think an article is Fake News or real reporting. You'll find the answer upside down at the end of each article.

Mystery Sausage-roll Lover Holds Giant Teddy to Ransom

A bear hunt is underway after a huge teddy bear was stolen from its perch on a Scottish street.

Rainbow, who was famous for his sign saying: 'Keep smiling', was last seen on Friday evening in Ardrossan, but his bear-nappers are now demanding a ransom of two sausage rolls to give him back.

The ransom note, which has been posted all over town, reads: 'We have your bear, Rainbow. If you want to see Rainbow again, bring two Greggs sausage rolls to the second green bench tomorrow at 11 a.m.'

Reports say that locals 'do not negotiate with terrorists', and so the hunt for Rainbow continues.

ANSWER: IT'S TRUE!

CLUES THAT MIGHT HELP YOU DECIDE IF THIS STORY IS REAL OR FAKE:

A. The article says that Rainbow has become quite well known in the town. You could try to find some articles about him online and maybe even a picture. If you find a reference to him online, then this story is more likely to be true.

B. The community seems to be coming together to try to find Rainbow. If so, the local newspaper might have interviewed some people who are trying to find him. If you can track down an interview from the paper or the paper's website then that will give you more vital information about the story.

CHOIR OF WASHING MACHINES TO OPEN HOUSEHOLD APPLIANCES CONFERENCE IN HONOLULU

A choir of sixty washing machines, dishwashers, microwaves, hairdryers and vacuum cleaners will be the star performers at the opening ceremony of this year's Household Appliances Conference.

First World War veteran, choirmaster and part-time repairman, Simran Sandhu, was tinkering in his workshop one afternoon when he made a startling discovery.

By devising a system of levers and pulleys, he realised he could make the machines turn on and off at exactly the right moments, with the resulting noises bearing a remarkable resemblance to 'Uptown Funk' by **BRUNO MARS**.

The choir's repertoire now features dozens of pieces, both pop and classical, and they have performed all over the world for celebrities and senior politicians.

Their most high-profile gig came in 1992, when the machines gave a haunting performance of one of Mozart's pianoforte concertos at a royal wedding.

Several of the dishwashers have recently collaborated with Canadian heart-throb **JUSTIN BIEBER** on his new single 'Gonna Wash You Outta My Hair'.

ANSWER: IT'S FALSE!

CLUES THAT MIGHT HELP YOU DECIDE IF THIS STORY IS REAL OR FAKE:

A. Does the Household Appliances Conference actually exist? Do a bit of digging and see. There are events like this all over the world, but there wasn't one being held in Honolulu in 2021, which is a pity because it sounds absolutely thrilling!

B. The article says that the choirmaster, Simran Sandhu, is a former soldier who fought in the First World War. If this were true, then Mr Sandhu would have to be over 100 years old. It's not impossible (some of your teachers might be nearing that age), but it's highly unlikely. You can use this clue to inform your decision about whether or not to believe the article.

C. A simple look through Justin Bieber's back catalogue (if you listen to his songs, make sure to wear earplugs) will tell you whether or not he released a song called *'Gonna Wash You Outta My Hair'* with a choir of washing machines.

WOMAN FINED FOR ATTACHING A LEAD TO HER HUSBAND AND TELLING POLICE HE WAS A DOG

A woman in Canada has been fined for trying to get around the rules designed to keep people safe during the coronavirus pandemic.

In the Canadian city of Sherbrooke, locals were told to stay indoors between the hours of 8 p.m. and 5 a.m., but people walking their dogs were exempt from the rule.

When police apprehended a couple who were out walking after 8 p.m., the woman refused to co-operate. She showed the police officers that her husband was attached to a lead that she was holding and insisted that he was not her husband, but actually a dog walking on two legs.

The police didn't believe her story and the couple were fined $1,546 – the equivalent of £893.

CLUES THAT MIGHT HELP YOU DECIDE IF THIS STORY IS REAL OR FAKE:

A. The article names a specific city in a specific part of Canada. Get your map out – is there such a city and is it where the article says it is? Some writers of Fake News don't bother with the details, so if you find that it's a real place then perhaps the writer is telling the truth.

B. The article is very precise about the times of day that locals are allowed out of their house. A quick search online should help you to find out if the government in that area did indeed impose a curfew between those times. If they're even an hour out, or you can't find any evidence of a curfew ever being put in place, then you should be wary.

C. At the end of the piece, the writer tells us how much the couple was fined in both Canadian dollars and British Pound sterling. That's a very precise number, suggesting that the writer has done their homework. You could check to see if $1,546 really DOES equal £893. Remember, though, sometimes those numbers go up and down, but usually only by small amounts, so it should still be pretty close.

MAN SUES HIS WIFE FOR REMOVING SIGN REMINDING HIM TO WEAR TROUSERS

A man from Austin, Texas, is taking legal action against his wife after she removed a sign from his bedside table that reminded him to wear trousers to work. He was then fired from his job.

Billy 'Bulldog' Mathieson, who worked at the Freedom Valley Aquarium in Seattle, Washington, claims that his wife, Cindy 'Bulldog' Mathieson, had been tidying their bedroom and threw away the 'LIVE. LAUGH. WEAR TROUSERS TO WORK.' sign that had been by his bed for thirty years.

On the morning in question, Mrs Mathieson was visiting her sister in New York and so she didn't realise that her husband hadn't put on the item of clothing.

'It wasn't until about three in the afternoon when my boss called me over and said, "Barry, you're not wearing any trousers!" I looked down and, gosh-darn-it, he was right!' Mr Mathieson told the court.

Mr Mathieson was fired and is suing his wife for damages.

However the case was thrown out of court this morning as Mr Mathieson had, once again, forgotten to wear trousers. As before, he blamed his wife and is expected to appeal the decision.

LIVE. LAUGH.
WEAR
TROUSERS TO WORK.

CLUES THAT MIGHT HELP YOU DECIDE IF THIS STORY IS REAL OR FAKE:

A. You're told that this man's name is Billy 'Bulldog' Mathieson. How likely is it that his wife is also nicknamed 'Bulldog'? Apart from not being a very nice nickname, surely it would become very confusing having two 'Bulldogs' living under the same roof?

B. You're given the name of an aquarium here and where it's located: Seattle. Is it likely that Billy 'Bulldog' Mathieson would get up in the morning, travel 2,116 miles from Austin, Texas, to Seattle, Washington, for work and then go home again? That doesn't sound believable.

C. Billy is referred to as 'Barry' later in the article. Small mistakes like that should set alarm bells ringing in your head.

SCIENCE HAS FINALLY FOUND OUT HOW MANY HOT DOGS A HUMAN CAN EAT AT ONCE

Scientists have just discovered the largest number of hot dogs, in theory, a human being can eat at once – eighty-four to be precise.

The current world record holder for most hot dogs eaten in one sitting is Joey Chestnut, who managed to gulp down seventy-five in ten minutes – nine short of equalling that amount.

The study, published in the American journal *Biology Letters*, analysed thirty-nine years of the annual US National Hot Dog Eating Contest. Researchers studied 'gut capacity' to work out how many hot dogs would fit into a human stomach.

CLUES THAT MIGHT HELP YOU DECIDE IF THIS STORY IS REAL OR FAKE:

A. The article says that Joey Chestnut is the world record holder for this astonishing feat. You can do some quick research here to find out if that's true. If Joey is indeed the world record holder, then he probably didn't keep it to himself. There may be well be other articles about him, or even an interview with Joey online.

B. There's a source mentioned in the article, which is often very helpful when you're trying to work out if a story is true or false. You should research the *Biology Letters* journal. If it's a widely known and respected journal, then you're probably reading real news. If, however, it's published from a teenager's bedroom and has a readership of three (including the editor's pet chinchilla), then you should be a lot more cautious.

C. Here's another event that sounds unlikely, a little like the Household Appliances Conference. Hop online and check it out. Are there videos of the competition happening? Does it have a convincing website? Are there any interviews online of people who have been there? With this story, there most certainly are.

News for YOU

What's news and what's not? Put your pals to the test and see if they can spot what's real and what's rubbish.

Find a story from a newspaper, magazine or website that makes you giggle or say:
'I can't believe that happened!'

Next, sit down and make up your own story. It can be as weird and wacky as you like. If you're struggling to come up with a fake story, here are some suggestions to help get you started:

AUSTRALIAN VOTERS ACCIDENTALLY ELECT KOALA BEAR AS MAYOR OF TOWN

MAN WHO TOOK LAXATIVE MEDICATION BEFORE BEING TRAPPED IN A LIFT FOR 14 HOURS 'GLAD TO BE OUT'

WOMAN WHO LOCKED HUSBAND IN THE GARDEN SHED OVERNIGHT INSISTS SHE 'THOUGHT HE WAS A BURGLAR'

Now read the real article to a friend and then your fake one and see if they can spot the difference. You'd be surprised how many people fall for the fake stuff.

If your pal fell for one of the fake stories, point out one or two things in the tall tale that give away that it's false. That will help them to be better prepared to sniff out Fake News the next time around.

REMEMBER: this is one of the few times you'll ever be asked to write Fake News and get away with it, unless you're planning a career in comedy!

SURPRISE STORY

Imagine you and your friends are in the middle of a huge game of hide-and-seek in the woods near where you live.

Your friend is counting down from a hundred, so you all scatter and sprint as fast as you can to your favourite hiding spots.

Disaster – they've all been nabbed already. You hear the sound of your friend's voice floating through the trees – she's coming closer! You twist your head this way and that, desperate to find a hiding place before she catches you.

There! A huge tree root is sticking up out of the forest floor, creating a tunnel of moss that you slide into. You grab some ferns and cover yourself with them . . . and wait.

Your friend's voice is growing fainter now. You think she might have missed your hiding place. The forest grows silent.

Hang on – your hand can feel something cold in the undergrowth. You peer down and take a look. It's an enormous flat boulder – you've been lying on it the whole time, cushioned by the moss.

You take a closer look. This isn't just a normal grey rock – its surface is streaked with a bright yellowish pattern. It's almost glowing, like a pot of . . . **gold?**

You brush away more moss and your jaw drops. Long patterns of this golden material snake all over the rock. It's definitely sparkling.

Could this rock actually be flecked with gold? Does anyone know it's here? Could it be worth something?

There's a story, all set and ready for you to investigate.

MAKING NEWS

Now that you know more about the news, how it works and how to tell what's real from what's rubbish, hopefully you're hungry to know about making and breaking real news and reporting news stories like a pro!

A Day in the Life of a 'Real News' Hound

For a **'real news'** hound, no two days are the same. Here's an example of a typical day of sniffing out the **TRUE from the POO**.

10 A.M. I arrive at the TV studios, just in time for the newsroom meeting. Our **editor** has been up since the crack of dawn, deciding what stories will be on our programme tonight. I'm assigned a story about elderly people receiving phone calls from fraudsters who try to steal their bank details. I'm told to have a two-minute television **package** ready for the programme at 6:30 p.m., so it's time to get going.

10 30 A.M. I hit the phones and start trying to find a **case study**. This a person who has been affected by the story, who will be my example to show the viewers what these scammers are doing.

12 00 P.M. We manage to locate an older gentleman close by who has been contacted by fraudsters over the phone. He's lost a lot of money so he's very angry and is willing to be interviewed so that other people don't fall for the same scam.

1 00 P.M. We arrive at our case study's house. He's a grandfather called Robert. We set up our camera, our lights and our microphones, and then I interview him about his experience and the money he has lost.

2 00 P.M. We leave Robert's house and drive straight to the headquarters of a charity, where we meet the people who are working to protect the elderly from scams. We film an interview with the chief executive, and she gives us some statistics (numbers) about how many crimes like this happen each year.

3 00 P.M. We arrive back in the newsroom and set to work getting the report ready for the programme. I choose the best clips from the interviews and start writing a script.

3 30 P.M. With my script ready to go, I head to a small sound booth in the newsroom and record myself saying it.

4 00 P.M. I visit the graphics department in the newsroom, which is full of very clever people who make computer-generated images and words. They'll take the statistics I noted down earlier and draw some fantastic illustrations that will spell out the facts and figures to the viewers.

5 00 P.M. The graphics wizards have sent me the illustrations of the statistics. I begin to glue everything together: the **voiceover**, the interview clips, the **stock shots** and the graphics. Before I know it, it's time for my news editor to watch the package and decide if it's ready to air.

6 00 P.M. DISASTER! My news editor phones me and tells me that the statistics we're using in the package aren't reliable – they could even be **FAKE NEWS** The programme starts in half an hour – **eeek!** I call the charity who gave us the statistics earlier in the day and they realise they've sent figures from ten years ago! They apologise and promise to send over the real numbers. That was a close one. Thankfully, my editor is always on the lookout for facts and figures that don't look right – they're an expert Fake News spotter.

6 27 P.M. I record a new voiceover, reciting the real statistics, and slot it into my report. I call my news editor to say the package is ready. If it hadn't been ready, there would have been a big gap in the news programme.

6 30 P.M. The programme goes on air and my report goes out with no problems. I breathe a huge sigh of relief.

7 00 P.M. When the programme is over, we have
another meeting. The news editor discusses what
went well, and whether there were any problems.
This is called a '**debrief**' and it's a very important
part of the day.

7 30 P.M. After dinner, I consider watching the news
before bed . . . but it's good to have some downtime,
so instead I watch three episodes of my favourite show
on YouTube (**shhh**, don't tell my editor – they might
think I should be watching the news all the time!).

CHAPTER 6

WHAT IS A STORY?

News reporters and journalists (AKA **newshounds**) are writers like any other – with one big difference. We don't make up amazing stories, we find *real* amazing stories and tell them to people. Our characters are REAL **PEOPLE**. Our heroes are REAL **HEROES**. Our villains are REAL **VILLAINS**.

Sometimes I dream up crazy-weird stories when I'm soaking in the bath, such as:

ALIEN ABDUCTION TAKES PLACE IN CANNED PEAS AISLE OF LIDL

OR

Ninety-six-year-old great-grandmother becomes billionaire after discovering a cure for hiccups

But there are amazing real stories just like these everywhere. So why would you make something up if real life is even more exciting and strange? A story can be funny, unusual, sad, surprising or even scary. Newshounds decide which stories matter. And believe me, stories are everywhere. So, get out of the bath, dry yourself off and let me take you on a fascinating journey to reveal how real news is created.

First things first, if we're talking about generating real news (not that fake stuff) we need to know the following . . . **da, da, DAAAAAH!**

'Real News' Hound Commandments

1. TELL THE TRUTH: It's important to be able to cut through all the jibber-jabber that we hear and see every day. Sometimes, the truth is like a needle in a box of needles on a lorry full of needles on the way to the World Needle Convention. In other words, it can be hard to find. If being a 'real news' hound reporter was easy, then everyone would be doing it because it sounds like an exciting job. Maybe (like that needle I lost at the World Needle Convention) the truth will never be found, but a real journalist tries their best.

2. BE FAIR: You've probably heard the phrase 'there are two sides to every story'. Being fair means listening to both sides. Some stories have three sides, some have ten and some have an endless number of sides. A great newshound doesn't have to tell everyone's side, but they'll report what they feel is important to the story. We'll talk more about this later.

3. STAY SAFE: When tracking down real news, you often get to go to exciting places and speak to amazing people. But sometimes you have to go to places you might not have been to before, such as crowded protests, farms, factories or the back of a moving horsebox at the Cheltenham Horseraces. It's important that newshounds never do anything that puts themselves or other people in danger!

4. BE CURIOUS: The world around us is full of stories. Put down this book and take a short stroll outside. I guarantee you'll see at least ten people, places or things that would make a great story. Finding amazing stories starts with having a curious mind. Asking a ton of questions might just lead to a really big, exciting story.

5. BE KIND: Be nice to folks. Online, in print or in real life. There are people behind every story. Every story means something to someone, every name is a person. Newshounds are some of the kindest people I've met.

MARIE COLVIN

Marie Colvin was instantly recognisable. Her eyepatch was legendary, as was the reason she wore it: she lost an eye reporting on violence in Sri Lanka.

She was born in New York and began her career writing for her university newspaper. Soon she was reporting on huge events in Washington DC, Paris, the Middle East and many African countries.

She was known for caring deeply about the people she interviewed, many of whom were living in war-torn countries or had experienced horrific violence. In 2012, after decades of travelling the world and telling the stories of thousands of people, she lost her life in the Syrian city of Homs.

> 'She was totally, totally committed to what she did – the importance of telling a story, of writing it. And getting it out to the world . . . that was her life.'
> – **Rosemarie Colvin, Marie Colvin's mum**

CHAPTER 7

STORIES ARE EVERYWHERE

Look out of the window. Or if you're outside, find a window and look into it (be careful you don't get caught!). Once you've found a window to look out of/ into, I promise you that you'll be looking at a story. Stories are **everywhere**. They might not be enormous, swashbuckling, eye-popping, jaw-dropping stories, but they're still stories.

Take a normal everyday situation: you're sitting doing your homework one evening when your next-door neighbour Camila, raps on the kitchen window, looking panic-stricken. You jump up (any excuse to take a break) and crack open the window.

'Have you seen Mr Tibbles?!' Camila yells. Her hair is in rollers and she's wearing her dressing gown outside in broad daylight, which isn't like her at all.

'Who?' you ask, poking your head even further out of the window.

'Mr Tibbles! My cat! I can't find him anywhere.' She's doing a little jig in panic.

You remember now – Mr Tibbles is a large, one-eyed cat that would win the prize for Most Unfriendly Feline in the World, if such a prize existed.

'No, I haven't seen him,' you tell Camila, who shouts at you and flounces back up the driveway.

You watch her go, dressing gown billowing dramatically in the wind, and then you shut the window firmly. As you sit back down to your maths homework, you're still thinking of Mr Tibbles.

The average person would think: 'Poor Mr Tibbles!'

A newshound would think: 'Poor Mr Tibbles! **Is this a story?**'

'Nonsense!' I hear you shout. It's just a missing cat. But before you rush to the bathroom and flush this book down the toilet (it won't flush by the way – many have tried and failed), think about what makes a story. For something to be a story, it has to matter to people.

Now, you might think: *'Who cares if an unfriendly moggie goes missing?'* Well, if any of your neighbours know Mr Tibbles, they might be concerned for his welfare. Maybe they have cats too – cats that could go missing for all sorts of reasons. How **unusual** is it for a cat to go missing? A few dozen in your town every year? And what about across the country? On other continents?

Across the world? Maybe, just maybe, there are **thousands** or even **millions** of missing cats whose owners still don't know what happened to them.

That's when you begin to ask questions – just to yourself to start with.

'Why do so many cats go missing?'

'Is there any way of making sure this doesn't happen to people's pets?'

'Are there more or fewer cats disappearing now than before?'

'Whose job is it to find these cats?'

'Are the cats really in trouble, or do they go missing because they fancy a change of scenery?'

These are all really good questions and once you start trying to find answers to them . . .

You're thinking like a journalist!

CHAPTER 8

TRUE, NEW AND MATTERS TO WHO?

So, you want to write a news story, but how do you decide whether or not it's important enough to spend your time on? Well, luckily, there's a really simple way of doing that.

All you have to ask is:

Is it TRUE?

Is it NEW?

It matters to WHO?

1. Is it TRUE?

As we know by now, this should be the first question you ask yourself when you hear about a story. If it's not true, it's not a story! Some fake stories are easy to spot, like a tale about an enormous man-eating trout living in the pond beside your house. It would be amazing if it were true, but unfortunately it's probably not.

2. Is it NEW?

Picture this: you've got a great story. Your English teacher has set a world record by eating the most hard-boiled eggs in a single sitting: 208 in one go! He was raising money for a new school roof, which is now being built. You've seen videos of him doing it and he's happy to be interviewed. So you know it's true. But is it *new*? You type his name into Google . . . oh dear. He ate that monstrous pile of eggs three weeks ago, and he's already been interviewed by several local newspapers and the local radio station. There was also a social media video with great shots of him stuffing mounds of hard-boiled eggs into his face (ew).Your story is true, but it's not new. Why would someone want to read your news article if you're telling them something they've already seen and heard?

Remember, there's a reason we call it 'news'.

Your story has to be NEW.

59

3. It matters to WHO?

Once you've found a story that is both true and new, the final question to ask yourself is: 'It matters to who?' This is when you decide whether or not it will be of interest to viewers, listeners and readers, whoever they may be. Think about where the story takes place, how many people are going to be affected by it and who they are.

The more people a story affects, the bigger it is. Your granny losing her false teeth down the sink is one thing. But if hundreds of grannies lost their false teeth down the sink and were wandering the streets of your neighbourhood like a plague of gummy elderly zombies, then that's a much bigger story.

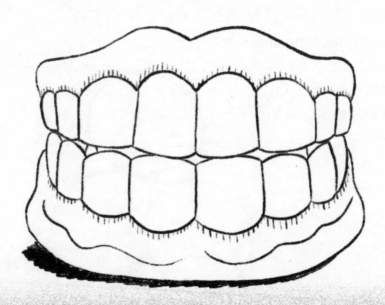

Our audience also cares about stories that happen close to them – a series of bicycle thefts in the local area, perhaps, or a family of racoons being introduced to your neighbourhood park. Because the story has happened close to where they live, they might even feel like they're part of it in a small way.

The most interesting stories are the ones that have happened close to where your audience lives **AND** affect lots of people. The least interesting stories are the ones that have happened far away from where your audience lives AND affect very few people.

So to illustrate this point with some ***FAKE NEWS ALERT*** imaginary examples, let's imagine you're working as a junior reporter at the *Mudford Buzz*, a UK online news outlet. You get four phone calls from four different people, all insisting that you simply must cover the stories they're telling you about. See which ones you think make the best stories:

CALLER 1

'I've got a brilliant story for you!
A truck on the way to Aoyama zoo
in Japan crashed on a motorway
and there are wild animals roaming
around the streets of Tokyo!
Elephants are overturning cars,
lions are eating schoolchildren,
monkeys are driving buses!
It's chaos!'

CALLER 2

'Hello, this is the Mayor of Mudford here.
I was in my study with my viola last night, practising for
the annual Mudford Small-But-Not-That-Small Stringed
Instruments Concert, when a mouse scurried in under the door.
I screamed the house down and gave chase with my viola. I swung
at him several times, smashing my small-but-not-that-small
stringed instrument to pieces, but I missed.
The blasted animal escaped!'

'Hello, can you hear me? I'm calling from Mozambique in South Africa. I thought the *Mudford Buzz* might be interested in something I've just heard. Apparently, a local woman from Chicualacuala made a pavlova while sleepwalking last night. She said she woke up standing in her kitchen, whipping her meringue into stiff peaks with a pot of strawberry jam bubbling on the cooker. Incredible stuff!'

'Good morning! This is Hiroshi Kitamaru, I'm the vet here in Mudford. There's been a bit of a mix-up at the surgery. We've had about two hundred dogs in for check-ups in the past week and instead of giving them regular pet treats, it seems we accidentally gave them a new and untested brand of dog biscuits called Zombiscuits. Many of them had a bad reaction and it's turned them all into vicious, man-eating monsters. They're probably eating their owners alive right now. Just thought I should let you know. Thanks, bye!'

One of these stories affects a small amount of people, close to where you live . . . **it's Caller 2**.

One of them affects a large amount of people, but quite far away from where you live . . . **it's Caller 1**.

One story affects a small amount of people, very far away . . . **it's Caller 3**.

But one of them affects a **LOT** of people, **VERY** close to where you live . . . **it's Caller 4**. And **THAT'S** the story that will be of greatest interest to your audience.

Here's another ***FAKE NEWS ALERT*** imaginary example. You've had your lunch (a delicious jellied eel quiche, of course), and you sit back down to your desk. Four emails have dropped into your inbox – all of them from people wanting you to write up a particular story. Which story do you think you should put on the front page of the *Mudford Buzz*?

From: B Sadiku
Subject: **Amazing news story!**
To: Nick Sheridan

EMAIL 1

Hello there,

I wanted to let you know about a story you might be interested in.

My nephew has just returned from Germany and told me the most remarkable story about his best friend's grandmother, Frau Ursula Dreyfus.

Mrs Dreyfus got up one morning and had a hearty breakfast of eggs on toast before realising, to her considerable distress, that instead of her own false teeth she had put in her husband's by mistake.

She only realised when she picked a tiny chunk of bacon from behind her back molar – Mrs Dreyfus is a vegetarian and so it dawned on her that there had been a mix-up.

Yours,
Mrs Bisa Sadiku

Hello,

I've just returned from a carol service at St Vivienne's Church in Mudford, round the corner from your website's offices. It was a lovely service. Mrs Ward gave a sublime performance of 'Santa Baby'. But as I got up to leave, I realised that the seat of my dress was quite sodden.

It turns out that some selfish individual had left a half-eaten pot of apricot yoghurt on the pew. I sat on it by accident and throughout the duration of the service it seeped into my dress. I'm most upset that someone would be so careless. I suspect Mrs Atkinson – she has a habit of eating yoghurts, pasties and the occasional roast chicken during church services.

Perhaps you could write an article about this incident? Maybe even install a hidden camera to catch Mrs Atkinson in the act?

Let me know if I can be of any assistance. Thank you.

Mrs Shveta Sekhon

From: E Fencery
Subject: **Cabbage Mayhem!**
To: Nick Sheridan

Hiya,

I'm on holiday in the small Swedish town of Lulea and there's just been an absolutely enormous explosion in the local cabbage factory. Flaming cabbages of all shapes and sizes rained down on the town, smashing car windscreens, exploding on the pavement and causing all sorts of mayhem.

One particularly large brassica landed on the main street, narrowly avoiding a group of schoolchildren on a class trip and leaving a huge smouldering crater.

Thankfully no one was injured, but it's probably the biggest thing that's ever happened in this town and it's already being referred to as 'The Great Lulea Cabbage Disaster'.

Do say if you need any more details.

Mr Emmet Fencery

Hi there,

I've been shopping in the Mudford branch of SuperSavers for over twenty years now – it's reasonably priced and the staff are very helpful. However, it was only a few weeks ago when I noticed that one of the ladies on the checkout, 'Bev', according to her name tag, bore a striking resemblance to rock-and-roll legend Elvis 'the Pelvis' Presley.

I thought that surely I must be mistaken, as Elvis has been dead for decades. But yesterday, as 'Bev' scanned through my shopping (canned sardines, toilet paper and a bottle of lemonade) she said I should be careful upon opening the lemonade as it had been 'all shook up'. I immediately recognised the name of Elvis's 1957 hit, and 'Bev' clamped her mouth over her mouth in horror.

She eventually confessed that she's not 'Bev' at all. Sick of the limelight and celebrity lifestyle, Elvis faked his own death in 1977 and smuggled himself into England. He disguised himself as a middle-aged woman and got a job in SuperSavers – where he has found the change of pace most refreshing. He goes to Mudford Bingo every Wednesday night without fail and he's also been very active in the Mudford Flower Arranging Guild.

He begged me not to reveal his secret, even attempting to bribe me with a £10 SuperSavers gift card, which I declined. The world must know: Elvis is not dead – he is Bev Chudley of 51, Churchill Court, Mudford!

Yours,
Mr Colin Ding

Remember, the basic idea behind deciding what story to write is working out which one affects the largest number of people, the closest to where your audience is. And in this example, it's most certainly Email 4. Journalists use this simple system to spot stories that they think their readers will be interested in. They also use it to filter out the stories that don't really matter to their audience.

All stories are important, but reporters and their editors only have a certain amount of time and space. Sorting out what's most interesting is a key skill for journalists.

CHAPTER 9

TOPLINES AND HEADLINES

Two phrases that newshounds use every day are 'topline' and 'headline'. They might sound similar, and sometimes they are, but they do mean slightly different things.

Both of them are ways of summing up a story in a short sentence. For example, the paragraph on the back of this book or a **DANGER** label on the front of a box of dynamite – they tell you the important information, without you having to open the book or prise open the box, blowing yourself to smithereens.

The biggest difference between a topline and a headline is when they're written and who they're written for.

Toplines

Once you've sniffed out a jaw-dropping story that will spread across the globe like wildfire, that's when you need to write your topline. This is a short sentence that will persuade news editors to run the story on their website, feature it in their news programme, or print it on their front page.

A topline should be so sharp and sizzling hot that a news editor will drop their jam doughnut and shriek:

'This is going to be the biggest story ever printed' or 'Our computers are going to explode because of all the traffic this story is going to bring to our website!'

Here are a few (imaginary) toplines that would make most news editors pop with excitement:

THE WRECK OF AN ANCIENT SPACECRAFT HAS BEEN DISCOVERED UNDER A SCHOOL CANTEEN.

OR

A LOCAL TRAPEZE ARTIST HAS GIVEN BIRTH TO OCTUPLETS, HALFWAY THROUGH A CIRCUS ROUTINE AT THE RACECOURSE.

The very **ESSENCE** of the story has been **squuuueezed** into a single short sentence that would make most people want to read more (especially the trapeze artist's husband).

But the same stories could have very boring toplines, if they're not written well, like:

A GROUP OF KIDS WERE PLANTING SOME HYDRANGEAS IN THE SCHOOLYARD LAST WEEK WHEN ALISON'S SHOVEL HIT SOMETHING HARD. THEY HAD A BIT OF A SCRABBLE IN THE MUCK AND THEN THEIR TEACHER CALLED THE LOCAL ARCHAEOLOGICAL SOCIETY. A GROUP OF EXPERTS CAME DOWN TO THE SCHOOL AND IT LOOKS LIKE THE CHILDREN DISCOVERED SOME SORT OF OLD AEROPLANE OR SOMETHING, SO THAT'S PRETTY COOL.

OR

A LOCAL WOMAN GAVE BIRTH AT THE WEEKEND.

The stories haven't changed, but the toplines have. A great topline doesn't ramble, it doesn't use vague words and it makes editors and other newshounds want to know more. When you pitch a news story, the very first question you'll be asked is:

'WHAT'S THE TOPLINE?'

News for YOU

Grab a piece of paper and figure out
the topline for each of these stories.

1

Dr Fabianna Montecristo is known to perform
remarkably swift brain surgeries. Two years ago, she
managed a record-breaking twenty-six brain surgeries in
one day. Yesterday she performed an operation on the
Mayor of Mudford, Felicity Coulter, who woke up from the
surgery now able to speak Mandarin. Dr Montecristo says
she hopes to one day perform three brain surgeries at the
same time – watch this space!

2

The Mudford Parish Council elections were held last
night. With an enormous turnout of twenty-two voters, we
now have a newly elected council. Despite a small scuffle
at the village hall, in which ex-council chairman, Fergus
Belvedere, was hit by a rotten egg, everything proceeded
without incident. Noor Salim was re-elected as chairwoman
for the third year running. Joy Johnson was elected
treasurer and 101-year-old Bartek Domaracka was elected
secretary – Bartek was so excited by the news that he had
a heart attack on the spot and had to be airlifted
to Mudford Hospital.

Headlines

Headlines are just like toplines, except it's the READER or VIEWER who sees them. They're the words that will grab a person by their collar and make them dive deeper into the story. They're also a chance to have a bit of fun – to make a clever play on words.

Headlines need to be **PUNCHY**. They're written in big bold letters above the story, so they have to deserve their place there. There's also limited space for them, so they need to be attention-grabbing, short and snappy.

Here are some of my favourite (real) headlines:

For a newspaper article about how Pope Benedict XVI was revealed as a secret Fanta-addict:

FIZZY POPE

When the former boss of Starbucks, Howard Schultz, announced he was considering running for president:

HOWARD SCHULTZ BRINGS A WHOLE LATTE TROUBLE

When Scottish football team, Caley Thistle, demolished a weak Celtic team:

UPER CALEY GO BALLISTIC, ELTIC ARE ATROCIOUS

A man facing jail for stealing a wig:

MAN WHO SNATCHED WIG WILL HAVE TOUPEE

But if you don't think your headline through, you might end up with some pretty awful clangers, like these (also real) headlines:

HOMICIDE VICTIMS RARELY TALK TO POLICE

MAN FOUND DEAD IN GRAVEYARD

ONE-ARMED MAN APPLAUDS THE KINDNESS OF STRANGERS

News for YOU

Here are two true stories that are crying out for some pun-tastic headlines. Why don't you grab a pen and paper and see what you can come up with?

'A Tennessee farmer grew an enormous pumpkin, weighing in at almost 500 kg (the pumpkin, not the farmer)! He then carved out the pumpkin, climbed inside and rowed it down a river.'

'The first ever heavy-metal knitting competition is being held in Finland, with competitors rocking out to Metallica as they try to knit sweaters.'

And here are some more real stories that have been reported by various newspapers over the years. Can you guess what the missing words in the headlines are?

1 The *Portland Press Herald* in the United States ran a story about oak trees producing huge amounts of acorns at seemingly random times, which was troubling New England residents, because they had to rake them all up. Why exactly they're producing too many nuts was a bit of a mystery.

HEADLINE: 'IT'S A BOOM YEAR FOR ACORNS, BUT WHAT DRIVES THE CYCLE IS A TOUGH ___ __ _____'

2 The Caterer website wrote an article about the success that pizza restaurants were having in the UK. They interviewed chefs and business owners about the best way to make pizza and how to achieve the perfect blend of ingredients.

HEADLINE: 'THERE'S NO BUSINESSES LIKE _____ BUSINESS'

3 The *Independent* ran a story about some unusual items which were found in the sewers of the Scottish town of East Kilbride, including a Winnie-the-Pooh toy, a pair of pants and a pair of false teeth. Scottish Water launched a new campaign to discourage locals from flushing such items down the drain, as it had dealt with more than 40,000 blockages in one year.

HEADLINE: 'SEWER BLOCKED BY A LARGE _____'

CHAPTER 10

KNOW YOUR SOURCES!

The person, place or organisation where news comes from is called a '**source**'. Without sources there aren't any stories, so they're super important for newshounds!

Think of information from sources as ingredients and imagine that instead of a news story, a journalist is going to make a big pot of delicious stew. Do you think they would rather:

Make a thick, rich stew that's full of buttery potatoes, creamy broth and beautifully tender beef?

OR

Cobble together a watery pot of rotten vegetables, lumpy gravy and suspicious gristly meat?

A news story will only be delicious if the reporter has great ingredients. And that's why they look for great sources.

A good way of knowing how rich, creamy and true information is, is to ask: **'Where did it come from?'** If you don't know, then you should put on your newshound trousers and find out.

These days there's an awful lot of bad ingredients swirling around, especially online in our newsfeeds and timelines. It can be hard to figure out what's a good source and what's a bad one, but there are a few ways to find out.

Just like you find out how delicious a stew is likely to be by leaning over the pot and giving it a good **SNiiiiifFF**, journalists can do the same with sources. (Wow, now I really want some stew . . .)

Whenever I come across a person, place, thing or event that I think might be a story, my news-brain kicks into gear. I'm then able to decide whether or not I want to put on my newshound running shoes and **chase it!**

The following are the usual sources for news stories:

1. PEOPLE

People can be fantastic sources, but they can also provide false information, even if they don't mean to. A 'real news' hound can decide whether they believe the story by thinking about the person who told them. Can they be trusted? If they borrowed something of yours, would they bring it back? If they offered to babysit your pet guinea pig for the weekend, would you trust them to look after it and not bring it on a crazy weekend to Las Vegas? Most people are perfectly trustworthy, but there are a few simple questions that you can ask to make sure.

Here's an example of a conversation between school friends:

NGOZI: I've got a brilliant news story for you! You know the pond behind our school? It's infested by giant man-eating trout!

'REAL NEWS' HOUND: Okay . . . how do you know?

NGOZI: Everyone at school is talking about it!

'REAL NEWS' HOUND: Have you seen one?

NGOZI: No, but other people have!

'REAL NEWS' HOUND: Okay, great, who?

NGOZI: Oblivia!

'REAL NEWS' HOUND: What an unusual name. Where can I find Oblivia? I need to interview her and make sure the story is true.

NGOZI: I don't know. She told my cousin's maths teacher, and the maths teacher told my cousin's mum, and my cousin's mum told my cousin and my cousin told me.

'REAL NEWS' HOUND: And we don't know where Oblivia is?

NGOZI: Someone said she left town because she saw the giant man-eating trout. I think she moved to Germany.

'REAL NEWS' HOUND: Has anyone else seen one?

NGOZI: Erm, no.

In this example, our **'real news'** hound should probably go down to the pond themselves and have a look for the man-eating trout. If they don't find one, then this probably isn't a news story – it's a story for a **comic book**! Ngozi might believe that the trout exists, but just like a detective, a great newshound will always try to find proof.

Not everyone is a good news source and a 'real news' hound knows that not every story they hear is true.

2. THE INTERNET

The internet is bursting with information – some of it true and some of it false. You may have a phone yourself. If you do, you've probably seen a lot of **clickbait** articles that look like this:

'STUDENT OBLIVIA ATTACKED AND EATEN BY 300 KG MAN- (AND WOMAN-) EATING TROUT!'

'YOU WON'T BELIEVE WHAT THIS PET GUINEA PIG GOT UP TO ON HOLIDAY IN LAS VEGAS!'

'YOU'LL CRY YOUR EYES OUT WHEN YOU SEE THIS TROUT AND GUINEA PIG GET MARRIED IN LAS VEGAS.'

Some clickbait articles are real, but a lot of them are fake. All the author of clickbait journalism wants you to do is . . . **click**. The more clicks the article gets, the better for the author. The writer of clickbait sees you, the reader, as a 300 kg trout that they want to reel in, even if the information they're giving you is fake.

3. OTHER NEWS STORIES

Previously reported news stories are often (though not always) a reliable way of finding out what's going on in the world around us.

Think about it: we wouldn't know about astronauts **landing on the Moon** unless a TV crew filmed it happening. We wouldn't know about the *Titanic* **sinking** unless newspaper reporters interviewed people who were there.

In a thousand years' time, if the human race hasn't been destroyed by ***FAKE NEWS ALERT*** an army of mutated man-eating trout, people will be able to look at news reports and articles about coronavirus and understand what it was like to live during our time.

If you want to find out more information about a subject, the chances are that a journalist or reporter has already written something about it. When I was asked to present a news report about the smelliest cheeses made in Britain, I found a whole series of newspaper articles on the topic, including the one on the next page from the *Telegraph* newspaper.

Journalists call this kind of information '**background information**', and it's a source like any other.

SCIENTISTS HAVE FOUND WHAT
THEY BELIEVE IS THE SMELLIEST CHEESE
IN THE WORLD. VIEUX-BOULOGNE, A SOFT CHEESE
FROM BOULOGNE-SUR-MER IN NORTHERN FRANCE, BEAT
FOURTEEN OTHER WHIFFY VARIETIES IN TESTS, INCLUDING
ONE SO SMELLY IT'S REPUTEDLY BANNED ON SOME PUBLIC
TRANSPORT NETWORKS.

Beware of BIAS

Using other news stories as sources can be a normal part of doing your research, but it's important to remember that just because something has been published, that doesn't mean it's completely trustworthy.

When a reporter is deciding whether or not a news article is a good source or a bad source, a big part of that decision is about judging whether there's any evidence of bias in the article.

Bias simply means that a reporter feels they have more in common with one side of the story than the other, and so they treat the other side unfairly. That second part is very important. Reporters often identify more with one side of the story and that's okay.

What's **not okay** is if they then treat the other side unfairly.

A good example of this would be a sports reporter who's writing a report about the final of the US Open tennis tournament. Can you tell if the reporter prefers one player over another?

Sporting News

Dismal Dodebier absolutely walloped by outstanding Ryan

British tennis player, Tom Dodebier, was absolutely trounced last night at the US Open Final, overcome by a relentless display of sheer magical genius from JJ Ryan.

Dodebier, who has had a dismal season, couldn't keep up with Ryan – surely the greatest Irish sportsperson to have ever lived.

Although he won by a tiny number of points, in an epic match which lasted over fourteen hours, it was clear to any spectator that Ryan was the undisputed superior player – serving backhands and forehands that sometimes reached speeds of up to 150 miles an hour. He padded around the court like a panther, ready at every turn to blast a perfect shot across the net at his opponent.

Dodebier played terribly. He had all the skill of a concussed badger trying to escape from a binbag and is, without question, the most shoddy, incompetent, hopeless, useless, ineffectual, dull-witted, brainless, moronic, doltish, pea-brained, pig-ignorant, scatter-brained, inept, witless and silly sportsman I have ever had the misfortune to watch.

This is quite an **exaggerated** example, but it's clear that the reporter in question feels they have more in common with JJ Ryan. Their criticism of Tom Dodebier, even when the match lasted so long and was so nail-bitingly close, is deeply unfair.

A **good newshound** who's researching (for example) an article on Dodebier's performance so far this year, will realise immediately that this is a **biased article** and not use it as a source.

Of course, there's nothing wrong with the above reporter being a JJ Ryan fan and writing about the match. But the problem comes when they begin to treat the other side unfairly. No matter what a journalist's personal feelings are, they should **NEVER** allow those feelings to overcome their journalistic sense of **fairness**.

In the United Kingdom, most journalists and news outlets realise the importance of fairness. They work hard to make sure that their coverage is as unbiased as possible. Sometimes they slip up, but they try to learn from those moments.

In other places, like the United States, for example, some journalists and some news outlets are more upfront about which side of the story they believe and which people they feel they have the most in common with.

Readers of certain publications and viewers of certain TV channels will probably know which side of the debate these journalists come down on – whether they support certain politicians, what priorities they have, which causes they believe in and which they don't.

These news outlets and journalists have every right to cover and publish what they think their audience cares about, but it's important that the audience knows that bias can sometimes paint an incomplete picture.

Here are a few easy ways to spot bias, wherever you are in the world and whatever stories you're following:

Ask yourself if all the sides of the story are being told. Are we hearing from all the voices that we should? If not, what voices are we missing? Why might that be?

If you read an article or see a report that you think might be biased towards one group or against another, have a look at some other work that the journalist has done. Do they often write about the same topics? And do they frequently come to the same conclusion?

Ask yourself if the headline of this story is telling us something that's actually new. Has anything new happened? Or has the journalist simply reheated an old story so that they can talk about the same subject again? Why do they keep returning to the same story?

Read coverage of the same event from a few different publications or watch coverage on a different TV channel. Are the reports different, depending on the outlet? What's different and why might that be?

CHAPTER 11

FINDING YOUR MOJO

Over the centuries, the tools that people have used to write news stories have changed many times. Stone tablets became feathers that were dipped in ink and used to scrawl across paper. Those feathers eventually became pens. Then came clunky typewriters that would break your foot if you happened to drop one. Typewriters gave way to increasingly sophisticated computers. Nowadays, most people have extremely powerful computers in their pockets – **their smartphones**.

Filming videos and recording sound for TV used to be a very complicated job, requiring special equipment. TV news crews would arrive at the scene of a story, unload their van and slowly set up the equipment. There would be a producer to keep everything organised, a video-camera operator, a sound engineer and a reporter.

Today, a phone can take very high-quality photos and record sound easily. These photos are so high-quality that you can put them straight on the news and viewers at home won't even know they've been taken on a phone. Some journalists ONLY use mobile phones to film entire news packages. This method, known as '**mobile journalism**' or **MoJo**, is becoming more and more popular. Maybe you might like to be a MoJo. All you need is a phone and good news-sense.

Using mobile phones also means that instead of relying on clunky cameras that take up a lot of room and have to be lugged to the scene of a story, reporters can make members of the public their camerapeople, meaning that **anyone** can potentially make and break news!

When a story is unfolding in a public place, you can bet that lots of folks will whip out their phones and start recording. They can capture amazing moments totally by accident – and it can make for fantastic videos. More and more news outlets are using these videos to tell viewers what's happened.

If a dog happens to get free from its owner and runs riot around a very posh and expensive pottery shop, there's a good chance someone in the shop will pull out their phone and start recording. And I don't know about you, but **THOSE** are the videos I want to watch.

This type of MoJo has a very complicated-sounding name: **User-Generated Content** or **UGC**. All that means is: **someone was there and they filmed it.**

UGC places the viewer smack-bang in the middle of the action.

They will **GASP!** as they see the dog breaking loose,

they'll **SQUEAL!** at the sound of the expensive pottery shattering

and they'll **GIGGLE!** at the man trying desperately to get his pooch back under control.

Without UGC, the only way to tell that story is to ask the viewer to **imagine** what happened and what it sounded like. That's not much fun and it certainly doesn't make for great viewing.

There are some very important things to remember about MoJo or UGC:

1. If you want to make use of some UGC, for example by putting it in an article or using a clip of sound from it, you **MUST** ask permission first. These photos, audio clips and videos belong to the people who recorded them. Before you use anyone's material, you should make sure that they're happy for you to do so. Taking someone else's content and using it without their permission is like taking their toothbrush or their wig and using it without permission. **They'll probably be annoyed!**

2. UGC is often really exciting footage, but it's a source like any other. 'Real news' hounds need to be absolutely certain that they can **trust** it. Sometimes people upload videos or photos to social media and pretend that they're something that they're not. **Remember: if you aren't sure that the UGC is what it says it is, then you must take extra care.**

3. Sometimes UGC can be upsetting. It could show moments of **violence** or have **bad language** in it. You wouldn't show a friend something that might upset them without warning them first, and in the same way we should be careful about what videos we share with our audience.

SURPRISE STORY

There's a big meeting being held tonight at your school – parents and teachers are coming together to discuss the amount of time students are given for lunch. A few parents think that fifteen minutes should be more than enough time for you to wolf down a sandwich and go to the bathroom. They've written to the head teacher and some teachers seem to agree.

You and your classmates are horrified at the prospect of only having fifteen minutes for lunch, after spending the morning in a stuffy classroom trying to figure out maths problems and learning about ancient civilisations.

You know that your mum gets a whole hour for her lunch break, but when you point this out to her, she says: **'Yes, but I have a very stressful job.'** Your teacher says the same thing, and when you ask if kids can go to the big meeting you're told: **'No, it's only for adults.'**

This strikes you as a bit unfair. Sure, your mum might have a stressful job, but has she ever tried to memorise all of

Henry VIII's wives? School is like a job for you and your classmates, and you think you deserve a proper lunch break. At the very least, you feel you should be included in the conversation instead of just being ignored!

You begin to ask yourself: 'What's a reasonable amount of time for a lunch break?' You search online and find a set of statistics about how long lunch breaks last in schools around Europe. Some of them take an hour for lunch – does that mean that they're taking their education less seriously? To find out, you search for the best-performing countries in Europe when it comes to exams. How long these kids take for lunch doesn't seem to affect their test results, **so why** shouldn't your school take an hour for lunch?

It sounds to me like you've got a great story on your hands. You could interview your classmates about how they feel. You could even try to do a video or phone interview with a pupil in another country about their lunch time. And to make sure that you're telling as many sides of the story as you can, you should interview your head teacher and maybe a couple of parents.

There's your story!

TELLING STORIES

What's the point of finding a great story if you don't tell anyone? Once a journalist has a brilliant **scoop**, there are lots of different ways for them to tell it.

REPORTER'S TOOLKIT

Every great newshound needs a great toolkit. Those of you who fancy becoming a hotshot news reporter and finding fantastic stories might want to consider assembling one of your own.

The most important tool every newshound needs is a curious mind, but if the local supermarket is sold out of them, these are some of the other tools that a reporter should get their hands on:

PEN

To write something down, you'll first need a pen. Many young reporters these days use their phones to write notes, but I refuse to do that. I love losing my pen and spending fifteen to twenty minutes trying to find another one!

PIECE OF PAPER

A pen without a piece of paper is like a brain surgeon operating with only a spoon as an instrument - she might be able to give it a go, but she'll probably make a bit of a mess. Again, some young reporters prefer their phones. I've scribbled notes on napkins, paper bags and a receipt for bouncy castle rental.

FAKE MOUSTACHE

Sometimes a newshound needs to disguise his or her appearance, especially when digging into an exclusive story that means they need to work in secret.

VOICE RECORDER

It's a good idea to have a voice recorder when interviewing someone for a story. Only the most talented reporters are able to remember entire conversations without getting anything mixed up, and if a reporter includes a quote that someone didn't actually say then they're writing Fake News! An interviewee should always be asked if they're happy to be recorded, and if they are, they need to speak loudly and clearly so that the voice recorder is able to pick up everything they're saying.

IDENTITY CARD

Who knows when you might meet an interesting person with a good story to tell? Great newshounds always have a card that they can give to interviewees to show that they're a real-life journalist.

NICK SHERIDAN, NEWSHOUND

EXPERT IN FINDING EYE-POPPING, JAW-DROPPING STORIES

JOURNALIST, AUTHOR, EXPERT NAPPER (PART-TIME WEDDING SINGER, SEE REVERSE FOR RATES)

A reporter's toolkit can contain all sorts of things –
a lot of everyday objects can come in useful when
hunting for stories. Other things will only be used
in very rare circumstances – like these ones.

You never know when you might need them!

SMALL PAIR OF SCISSORS
(for trimming nose hair and toenails on the go)

SPARE PAIR OF PANTS
(for long nights staking out secret locations)

DICTIONARY
(for reading on long car journeys)

BREEDS OF
NEWSHOUND

Just like there are many different types of doctors, teachers and trombone-players, there are also lots of different types of newshound. Some of them are sent out by editors to track down specific stories and some of them sniff the news out by themselves. Just like with other hounds, it's important to get the right sort of newshound for the job – after all, you wouldn't ask a Chihuahua to be a police dog.

GENERAL REPORTERS

These journalists will try anything – every day is different for them. One day they're snorkelling with dogs in a local outdoor swimming pool, the next they're interviewing the world's first accordion-playing heart surgeon. This is often where young newshounds start their careers.

BUSINESS JOURNALISTS

These journalists have super-computer brains that help them to make sense of endless numbers and mountains of spreadsheets that other reporters might struggle to get their heads around.

SPORTS JOURNALISTS

Some people think that all sports journalists do is sit around and watch sports. That is part of their job, but then they have to write articles and carry out interviews too, so there's a lot of work involved. They need to have an interest in all sorts of sports. That means they don't just watch the Champions League Final, but also things like skateboarding, tennis, trampolining, snooker, archery, synchronised swimming, deer-stalking, chess, yodelling, Cluedo, the National Haggis-throwing Championships, and ancient videos of Athlone Town FC playing against AC Milan in 1975.

INVESTIGATIVE REPORTERS

Investigative reporters usually have many years as general reporters under their belts. They often tell stories about big organisations that treat people unfairly or something that a government has been doing wrong for a long time.

ENTERTAINMENT REPORTERS

Entertainment reporters spend their time jetting off to exotic locations, meeting movie stars and walking the red carpet, finding stories, interviewing people, writing articles and filming TV reports. But, like a sports journalist, they need to work very hard – for every Oscars ceremony that they go to, there's a village hall panto to review. No story should be too big or too small for a great entertainment reporter.

CHAPTER 12

THE FIVE Ws AND ONE H

Some questions are more important than others. An example of a not-very-important question might be 'How dare you use my egg-and-cress sandwich as a bookmark?' or 'Why are you late this morning, Sheridan?!'

The best news stories require us to ask important questions and the most important questions of all begin with the letter '**W**' and one '**H**' . . .

They are: **WHAT**, **WHEN**, **WHERE**, **WHO**, **WHY** and **HOW**.

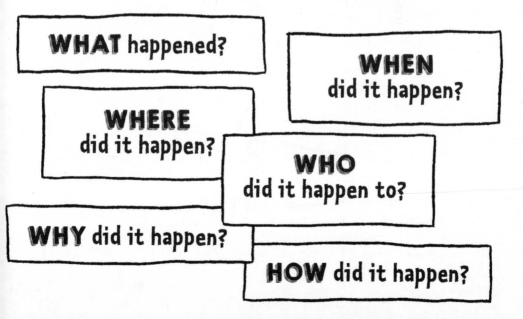

WHAT happened?

WHEN did it happen?

WHERE did it happen?

WHO did it happen to?

WHY did it happen?

HOW did it happen?

If you ask these questions and nothing else, then you have the beginnings of a news story. For example, let's take a **MADE-UP** story and see where the five W and one H questions are lurking.

POT-BELLIED PIG RUNS RIOT THROUGH NEWSPAPER BUILDING

Journalist Nick Sheridan has apologised to colleagues after his pet pot-bellied pig ran riot through his ninth-floor workplace yesterday morning.

Sheridan has admitted that the idea of bringing Stephen the pig to the office was 'perhaps not very well thought through', but insisted he had no choice due to his pig-sitter cancelling at very short notice.

Stephen snapped his lead and terrorised numerous members of staff. He's reported to have 'aggressively nibbled' several employees and helped himself to a box of strawberry-cream chocolates, which Linda had brought in for the treat table.

After over an hour of pig-based chaos, Stephen was eventually overpowered by the office receptionist. Sheridan declined to comment this morning, but it's understood that he's on his final warning from management following yesterday's events.

N.B. This article is a reminder to us all about the importance of accuracy. The journalist who wrote it made the mistake of writing that Stephen ate Linda's strawberry-cream chocolates – I know for a fact it was actually a boxful of treacle tartlets.

WHAT?

A pot-bellied pig called Stephen ran riot
through a workplace.

WHEN?

Yesterday morning.

WHERE?

A ninth-floor TV newsroom.

WHO?

Nick Sheridan.

WHY?

Nick's pig-sitter had to cancel at late notice.

HOW?

Stephen broke loose from his lead.

As you can see, the five W questions and one H
question are vital. If you decide to write a story but
first need to collect information from sources, make
sure that you keep asking these six questions.

They're a bit like the skeleton of the story: once you
have them in place, you can start asking more questions
and adding on the muscle, flesh, skin and all the other
parts like the wobbly bit at the bottom of your ear.

News for YOU

See if you can find the five Ws and one H in this MADE-UP story:

POLICE HUNT DISGRUNTLED EMPLOYEE IN CAR WASH DESSERT FIASCO

Police are searching for a former employee of Sudsy's Car Wash, believing him to be behind a series of dessert-based pranks at the business. Customers have had their cars sprayed with a variety of puddings, which owner Jim Sudsy insists must have been secretly poured into the tanks feeding the hoses.

'Employees have switched on the pumps, pointed the hose at the customer's car, and instead of a jet of hot water, they get a jet of pudding!' he said last night.

'This month alone, cars have been drenched with chocolate mousse, tiramisu, custard, low-fat mango gelato, hot fudge and a lumpy brown substance, which I suspect was chocolate-and-pomegranate cake with lavender ruffle frosting.'

Mr Sudsy believes that a former employee, Denis Peach, who was sacked last year for stealing disinfectant, is behind the pranks. Mr Peach is a trained pastry chef, which Mr Sudsy says clearly implicates him in the crimes.

'I've had his rhubarb-and-pistachio pavlova – he brought it to a staff party last year – and he knows what he's doing when it comes to pudding. But he needs to keep his desserts in the kitchen and out of my hoses!'

CHAPTER 13

INTERVIEWS AND VOX POPS

Interviews are really just conversations that journalists have in order to find out information. Some interviewees love the attention and it can be difficult to get them to stop talking. Other interviewees won't like it at all and it will be hard to get them to start talking. And sometimes people will want to talk a lot about one subject, but not so much about another.

I **love** talking about the mysterious disappearance of pilot **AMELIA EARHART**, who, in 1937, vanished over the Pacific Ocean while trying to become the first woman to fly around the world. I can easily talk for hours about her adventures (eight hours and forty-one seconds is my record – at my aunt's Christmas dinner party last year). But I **hate** talking about pot-bellied pigs, especially ones called Stephen.

Your head teacher might love talking about the brand-new library that's just been built in your school, but might not want to talk about how the gravy in the canteen has lumps with legs floating around in it.

Your mum or dad or guardian might love talking about how important it is to do your homework, but if you ask them to raise your pocket money they might become very quiet all of a sudden.

The trick to bagging a great interview is simple:

**you need to ask the right question
to get the right answer.**

Politicians, in particular, don't like answering difficult questions. Or maybe it's fairer to say that they have a prepared script and they want to stick to it!

In the run-up to elections, politicians are pushed into TV studios and forced to answer questions. For some reason, we use cooking words when we describe interview situations like this. Politicians are said to be 'grilled', 'roasted' and sometimes 'left stewing'. I've never tasted politician before, so I really don't understand why we use these words.

If a person doesn't want to answer a question, they probably won't lie. Instead, they'll try to avoid answering altogether.

A very smart man called Professor Peter Bull has actually come up with a list of ways for people to avoid answering difficult questions. **DOZENS**, in fact.

'Ridiculous!'

you might shout and fling your copy of this book out of the nearest window (its corners are quite sharp, so please wait until you're sure there's no one directly underneath).

'There can't be dozens of ways to avoid a question!'

Well, read this interview below and tell me what you think. The question being asked here is that famous old chestnut: 'Which came first, the chicken or the egg?' If someone (for example, a chicken farmer) didn't want to answer that question then the conversation might look something like this:

REPORTER: I finish by asking you which came first, the chicken or the egg?

FARMER: *(ignoring the question)* I love eggs, especially scrambled eggs.

REPORTER: But which came first?

FARMER: *(recognising the question but not answering it)* That's a really good question, and I love eggs, especially scrambled eggs.

REPORTER: And which actually came first?

FARMER: *(avoiding responsibility)* I'm not going to comment on a private matter between the chicken and the egg.

REPORTER: I just want to know which came first?

FARMER: *(saying the question is wrong)* It's not about which came first, it's about which tastes better!

REPORTER: We're running out of time, please
just tell me which came first!

FARMER: *(saying the question is pointless)* I'm not
going to sit here and speculate wildly about chickens
and eggs!

REPORTER: Last chance! Which came first, the chicken
or the egg?

FARMER: *(leading the interview completely off topic)*
If it wasn't for all these ducks coming over here then
everything would be fine!

This farmer is evidently a bit of a slippery customer
and he knows how to avoid answering questions.

News for YOU

TRY IT YOURSELF

Using Professor Bull's methods, pick a pal and ask them to see if they can squeeze an answer out of you based on the following super-difficult questions.

Are zebras black horses with white stripes or white horses with black stripes?

Aren't all mirrors 'used', even when you buy them new?

Is the colour orange named after the fruit or is the fruit named after the colour?

If you're preparing to interview someone, write down a list of questions beforehand. Some great interview questions might be:

'Can you start at the beginning and tell me what happened?'

'How did that make you feel?'

'Why do you think that?'

'Why is this so important to you?'

'Where can I find out more about this?'

'What's going to happen next?'

Try to avoid asking closed questions that can be answered with a simple '**Yes**' or '**No**'. An interview with someone who just answers 'Yes' or 'No' every time is a very boring one.

If you ask: 'Did the pot-bellied pig make you feel frightened?', then Linda might answer: 'Yes'. But if you ask an **open** question like: 'How did the pot-bellied pig make you feel?', then Linda might answer: 'I was absolutely scared out of my wits!' – and that's much more exciting.

Even though you have a list of questions prepared, don't forget to listen to what the person is telling you and add in questions that you haven't written down. Sometimes, reporters don't listen to their interviewees because they're too concerned about asking the next question on their list. An example might look something like this:

LOCAL DOCTOR'S LABORATORY DAMAGED BY ENORMOUS STORM

An interview with local doctor and general oddball Victor Frankenstein.

REPORTER: Dr Frankenstein, thanks so much for speaking to us today.

DR FRANKENSTEIN: Thank you for having me.

REPORTER: We're standing in your laboratory, which was very badly damaged in last night's bad weather. Thunder and lightning for hours!

DR FRANKENSTEIN: Yes, it's absolutely terrible. I really hope my insurance will pay out. Windows smashed, tables overturned, the ceiling has caved in, water everywhere – I'm not sure if it will ever be the same again.

REPORTER: Was anybody injured when the roof collapsed?

DR FRANKENSTEIN: Thankfully not. I managed to duck out of the way and shelter under a particularly large corpse that I had been disassembling for my latest creature.

REPORTER: How long will it take you to rebuild the lab?

DR FRANKENSTEIN: That's a very difficult question to answer. Thankfully, I have a lot of help. I've managed to build over twenty zombies from various dead bodies over the years, so they'll be happy to lend a hand. As long as I ask them nicely, I'm sure they won't throttle me to death *(chuckles)*.

REPORTER: Is there anything you'd like to say to the local community?

DR FRANKENSTEIN: Oh, yes. I've been digging up corpses from the local graveyard for the last decade, but unfortunately the supply is now running quite low. If any resident is reading this and thinks that an elderly relative is about to croak, would they please let me know and perhaps I can speed up the process a bit. They can write to me at: Dr Victor Frankenstein, The Laboratory, The Huge and Scary-looking Castle, Darmstadt, Germany.

REPORTER: Thank you very much for speaking to us Dr Frankenstein.

DR FRANKENSTEIN: My pleasure.

I'm sure you've been able to spot a few pieces of information that this young reporter ignored. They were so focused on their list of questions that they weren't listening to what the interviewee was saying. That poor reporter probably didn't make it out of Frankenstein's castle alive.

The lesson here is:

listen to what the interviewee is saying!

News for YOU

Here's a quick game you can try with your pals to test your listening skills.

Arrange yourselves in a circle. Pick someone to ask a question. For example, 'How did the lightning storm make you feel?' The person to their left says, 'The storm made me feel scared.'

The next person repeats the first answer and adds their own: 'The storm made me feel scared AND nervous'. The next person repeats the previous answers and must add to it again. Go round and round the circle for as long as you can, with everyone adding an answer each time.

LOUIS THEROUX

Louis Theroux might appear to be a mild-mannered, quietly spoken Brit, but nothing could be further from the truth. Well, he is British, but underneath that polite shell is a wildly intelligent journalist with a laser-sharp eye for news.

Louis is a master at making his interviewees feel comfortable. He connects with them in a very human way, which is super important for newshounds to do. He works mainly in television documentaries, travelling to the wildest and weirdest locations and talking to fascinating people.

Some of his interviewees have very different opinions to his own, but he doesn't let that get in the way of his journalism. If you want to make amazing documentaries, then Louis Theroux's work is the gold standard.

'We have evolved as living creatures
to express ourselves, to be creative,
to tell stories.'
– Louis Theroux

Vox Pops

'**Vox pop**' is a fancy Latin way of saying 'the voice of the people'. When my first news editor told me to 'Go get some vox pops', I thought I was being sent to the shop for a delicious sweet treat on a stick. I was very disappointed to learn that I was actually being sent out to wander up and down our local high street, interviewing **Joe** and **Josephine Public** about a news story.

'Joe and Josephine Public' aren't real people – it's a **phrase** that journalists use sometimes to refer to **ordinary folk**. So if a journalist says: 'What do Joe and Josephine Public think about this?' that means they're wondering if **normal**, everyday people have an **opinion** on a news story, and if so what it is.

Sometimes, journalists don't need to know what 'Joe and Josephine Public' think about a story. For example, if they were writing about how the world's lesser-spotted toad population has dipped slightly, they probably wouldn't need to ask the public about their opinions.

Why? Because ordinary people most likely don't know much about the lesser-spotted toad, and their decreasing population probably **won't affect them**.

But if they were writing a story about the price of a bus ticket in town going up by a pound, then 'Joe and Josephine Public' might very well have something to say about that! Or if they were filming a TV report about a local park being covered over by cement to make way for a block of offices then, again, ordinary people **probably** have opinions.

That's when a journalist decides to do some vox pops (i.e. interviewing 'Joe and Josephine Public' about the story). Vox pops are a great way of finding out about the '**mood on the ground**' – how a story comes across to everyday folks.

News for YOU

Here are a few examples of some MADE-UP vox pops that I've imagined took place at famous moments in history.

Have a read and see if you can guess what news story they're speaking about.

1 GLASGOW – SEPTEMBER 1945
Belinda Boggins, hairdresser:

'We just heard about it on the radio and we couldn't believe it! I was in the middle of doing Maggie Carberry's perm and I accidentally shaved her eyebrows off! It's been a long six years, so we're delighted to finally have some good news. We'll be having a huge party tonight at the salon. Though I don't think Mrs Carberry will be coming . . .'

2 LOS ANGELES – NOVEMBER 2008
Pandora Ora, school teacher:

'Wow – I honestly can't believe that he's going to be leading the country. It will mean a lot to the young people that I teach, and I hope it'll encourage kids everywhere to dream big. I think he's very charming, his wife and kids seem terrific and I hope he'll do a lot of great things for this country. Yes we can!'

ANSWER 2: Barack Obama is elected as the first Black president of the United States

ANSWER 1: The end of the Second World War

3 LONDON – MAY 1536
Charlie Stevens, stablehand:

'I thought it was all a bit harsh really. I've often had arguments with my wife, but I've never thought about doing what he's done. I suppose that means he's free to move on to the next one, whoever that is. If he came near my wife, she'd run a mile, and she'd be right too! Apart from everything else, I really can't stand his beard!'

4 WASHINGTON DC – APRIL 1865
Annie Cahill, dressmaker:

'It's such an awful shame. I always thought he was quite tall and handsome. I don't know who on earth would want to do him any harm at all. My sisters were in the front row when it happened and they said it was the loudest bang they've ever heard. I hope they get a refund on the tickets, it totally ruined their night out!'

ANSWER 4 : Abraham Lincoln is shot in a theatre

ANSWER 3: Henry VIII's second wife, Anne Boleyn, gets the chop

5 A SWAMP – 10,111 BCE

Ug, part-time caveman, part-time painter:

'Yes, I think it'll make an enormous difference to my life. I wasn't so sure at first, but it's cut down my morning commute from about ten hours to forty minutes. That means I can get to work quicker and there's less chance of me being attacked by a woolly mammoth or a sabre-toothed tiger. So, all in all, I can see this really catching on.'

Remember there's a difference between a vox pop and an eyewitness account. A vox pop is an interview with an ordinary member of the public who didn't play any part in the actual news event itself. An eyewitness is someone who saw what happened with their own eyes.

ANSWER 5: The invention of the wheel

CHAPTER 14

THE INVERTED PYRAMID

'**Inverted**' is just a fancy way of saying '**upside down**', and we rarely use the word in real-life conversations. When your friend hangs by her legs from a set of monkey bars, you might look at her and say: *'Oh, look, Cordelia is upside down.'* It's very unlikely that you would say: *'Oh, look, Cordelia is inverted.'*

It might sound a bit boring, but the 'inverted pyramid' is probably the most important part of writing a news story. It's a way of cracking the code and drawing the reader in by **showcasing** the most important information up front.

The inverted pyramid has nothing to do with ancient Egypt, which is a pity because the Egyptians were pretty cool. They didn't make their pyramids upside down because, let's face it, an upside-down pyramid wouldn't be very practical. Journalists do turn pyramids upside down, though, because instead of using huge blocks, they're using words.

Here's an upside-down pyramid:

Think of this as a news story that's being written. You'll notice that the widest part of the pyramid is at the top, and the narrowest at the bottom. When newshounds write stories, we put the most important information at the top and the least important information at the bottom.

If the pyramid was in its usual position, like this one, then the news article would have the least important information at the beginning (which would be a bit daft) and the most important information would be left until the end (which would also be daft).

Let's look at an example. In the first version of this **MADE-UP** report, the newshound has written a story with their pyramid the '**right**' way up, like this:

ASTRONAUT THINKS HIS EGG-AND-CRESS SANDWICH MIGHT HAVE GONE OFF

World-renowned astronaut, Kenneth Bacon, has told reporters that an egg-and-cress sandwich, which he ate while on a fact-finding mission to the planet Mars, might have gone off.

Speaking last night, Mr Bacon said: 'I didn't notice anything wrong at the start, but after a couple of bites, I began to feel a bit squiffy. I checked the expiry date on the sandwich, and although it said October ninth, the eggs were much too smelly to be fresh.'

While on the mission to Mars, Mr Bacon also discovered a colony of aliens, who told him that they would shortly be launching an enormous military attack against planet Earth.

As you can see, this reporter has left the most important and interesting piece of news until the end of the article. Planet Earth is about to be attacked by an army of aliens, and this article spends most of its time talking about a suspicious egg-and-cress sandwich.

If the reporter had used the '**inverted pyramid**' way of writing, then the news article would have looked something like this:

VICIOUS ALIENS ABOUT TO ATTACK PLANET EARTH

A huge army of aliens from Mars is preparing to launch an enormous attack on Earth, according to a world-renowned astronaut.

Kenneth Bacon, who has just returned from a fact-finding mission on Mars, told reporters last night that he came across a colony of Martians who are hell-bent on destroying earthly civilisation as we know it.

While on the mission, Mr Bacon also ate an egg-and-cress sandwich, which he thinks may have been past its expiry date. He had an upset stomach as a result.

In this article, the news reporter has put the most important information at the top. You might even think that the detail about the egg-and-cress sandwich is so unimportant that it shouldn't even be in this article – and you'd probably be right.

The inverted (or upside-down) pyramid is a way of helping us to decide what to put at the beginning, in the middle and at the end of a story. Whether you're writing an article, producing a TV news bulletin, or chatting to your friends, it's a great way of knowing what to say first and what to say last.

CHAPTER 15

WHERE A STORY GOES TODAY

RADIO

I was once told I have a '**good face for radio**'. Although I was very flattered at the time, I realised afterwards that the person wasn't paying me a compliment (*thanks, Dad*). Radio is one of the most popular forms of media in the world. People listen when they wake up; they listen while they burn their toast; they listen in their cars; and they listen in the bath.

There are lots of cool and interesting ways to become involved in the audio world. But being a radio journalist is a very challenging job, because you can't rely on photos or videos to tell the story to the audience.

Radio journalists have to paint a **picture for people's ears** (not literally, of course, as everyone knows that ears have notoriously poor taste in art). They do it using all sorts of sounds: voices, music and sound effects. They build the atmosphere using birdsong, the sound of traffic, rain falling on a roof, whatever they can think of to propel the story through the speaker and into the listener's brain.

Just like a TV newsroom, a radio newsroom has lots of different types of journalists. There are **radio newsreaders** who bring the very latest **breaking news** to listeners every hour. There are **reporters** who go out, armed with their recorders, tracking down stories and interviewees, sending back audio files from tiny laptops. And there are **journalists** working on full-length programmes, like podcasts and documentaries, doing research and recording long interviews.

TELEVISION

Television news is my favourite kind. Every TV report I make feels like a little two-minute film, and there are endless opportunities to be creative and to make viewers sit up and pay attention. TV journalists are newshounds like any other and there are loads of **different types**:

1. RESEARCHERS

Researchers work with **news reporters** and **anchors** to gather the most sizzling, red-hot information. They're **super-intelligent** people whose job it is to know **amazing** facts right off the top of their heads. Which footballer has scored more Champions League goals than any other? How many Eurovision Song Contests have there been? Who is the oldest person to have ever bungee-jumped off a cliff? Researchers find information and spread it around the rest of the newsroom. Many young newshounds start off their careers as researchers.

2. REPORTERS

TV reporters are people that you sometimes see on the news, standing **outside courtrooms**, or maybe on a clifftop **shouting** through a blustery storm or **yelling questions** at slimy businessmen trying to escape down an alleyway. Every day is different for them. When they arrive in the newsroom, they're given a story by their **editor** and told to make a television package by their **deadline**. They go out with a **cameraperson** and interview people, race back to the newsroom, put the package together on some sort of video-editing software and then watch it go out on the main evening news. The next day, they do it all over again. This is how I spend a lot of my time.

3. CAMERAPEOPLE

Camerapeople make the videos you see on the screen – without them, there is no TV news bulletin. Years ago, reporters used to go out and film interviews with huge crews: a cameraperson, a lighting person, a sound person, a driver – but not any more! These days the camerapeople do EVERYTHING. They're the ones you sometimes see running around with big camera kits on their shoulders. They very rarely get the credit they deserve, but their job is to tell the story as best they can through videos. Most importantly of all, they make the reporter look good, so regularly feeding them chocolate biscuits is a good idea.

4. PRODUCERS

Reporters can be very busy people so a good producer is someone who makes their lives less stressful. While a reporter is out filming with a cameraperson, a producer could be making phone calls trying to find more interviews, writing a script for the reporter, coming up with graphic pictures if statistics and numbers are needed and finding news footage that could help tell the story.

5. EDITORS

The editor is the boss of the newsroom. TV editors decide what stories will go in the evening programme and they choose which reporters will work on each story. They're usually very experienced and intelligent journalists. Most of them are perfectly lovely people, but if a journalist misses their deadline, then they might be a little less friendly!

ONLINE

Chances are, if you want to find out what's happening in the world right now, you'll go on the internet. Journalists who put their stories on the internet are just like those who work for TV programmes, radio shows and newspapers.

The internet is home to literally millions of news stories, and users need to keep their wits about them when looking online. As virtually anybody can post an article on the internet, there's more risk of Fake News making an appearance. We should only believe stories that are from '**reputable**' sources – that's sources that can be trusted to tell the truth and **ONLY** the truth.

There are some fantastic things about being an online journalist.

1. NEWS AT THE SPEED OF LIGHT

Online journalists don't need to scribble down their stories, send them to their boss, then wait for them to be sent to a factory to be printed on to huge pieces of paper and then delivered to shops the following day. Once they've written a great article, fact-checked it and made sure their editor is happy with it, all they have to do to catapult it into the world is hit '**PUBLISH**'.

The same rules apply to online journalism and print journalism – the story needs to be true, well-written and fair to everyone involved. But the internet cuts out an awful lot of the awkward in-between bits. You don't need a printing press, a delivery van, or even a shop shelf to put the newspapers on.

2. ALL THE SPACE YOU NEED

When a newspaper reporter writes a story, they need to keep within what's called the '**word count**'. That's how many words are in the story. If their boss asks them for a three-hundred-word story about a woman who fell off the stage at a local amateur dramatics performance, they don't want a thousand words. That's because a newspaper only has a certain amount of space. Online journalists don't need to worry about that. They can write as many words as they feel the story deserves – after all, there's plenty of room on the internet!

3. LOTS OF PEOPLE READ YOUR JOURNALISM

People love reading their news online. And why wouldn't they? All you have to do is open an app on your phone and you can read about alligators in Azerbaijan, politicians in Peru and throat-warblers in Mozambique. That means that stories by online journalists are read by millions of people, in some of the most wonderful places around the globe. If someone has internet access, then no matter where they are, they can read the words you've written and the stories you're telling. That's pretty cool.

LYSE DOUCET

If you've ever watched BBC News, particularly news reports from other parts of the world, you might have seen the face and heard the voice of Lyse Doucet.

She was born in Canada and has travelled the world reporting in some of the most far-flung and awe-inspiring locations. She makes television and radio reports that look at the impact of conflict and natural disasters on ordinary people like you and me, as well as people trying to escape from violence in their home country.

She always relays these stories in easy-to-understand language and her reports make you feel like you've been pulled through the television screen and are seeing these events with your own eyes and hearing the interview with your own ears. She's presented documentaries on extraordinary girls and women and has won dozens of awards for her reporting. Keep an eye out for her the next time you're watching the news – she rocks!

> 'I'm proud of every story that tells people something they didn't know, or changes their mind about something they do know.'
> – **Lyse Doucet**

SOCIAL MEDIA

News doesn't just live on news websites; it can also show up on social media. Many platforms like TikTok, Facebook, Twitter, Instagram and Snapchat are only open to people over the age of thirteen. Some are only available to those over the age of sixteen.

Even if you're not yet old enough to use these social media apps yourself, you might well do so in the future. So it's important to be prepared for some of the stuff you might see on your timelines in a few years' time.

Social media can be a handy way to learn about the news of the day – why install a special app on my phone when I can just follow a news outlet on social media and let stories appear on my timeline?

But it's important to remember that if someone shares a news story on their feed, they're likely to post it with some sort of **comment** or **reaction**. This can colour the way we view a story, and it might even tempt us to share the article ourselves or comment underneath without even reading it.

The person who posted the story might write:

'THIS PROVES THE GOVERNMENT HAS PUT WEIRD CHEMICALS INTO OUR WATER!'

or they might say:

'YET ANOTHER SCIENTIST SAYS THAT CLIMATE CHANGE ISN'T REAL!'

This is a great opportunity for us to put our newshound hats on and do some investigating ourselves.

Read the article and ask yourself about the five Ws and one H. Can you find them in the story? Are you convinced by the quotes? Look at the sources and ask yourself if you trust them.

Social media can be a brilliant tool to help journalists find stories, but the more time I spend scrolling, the more opportunity there is for me to encounter **unfriendly people**. People say nasty things online that they would never say in real life.

There are a few reasons for this. One is that social media gives mean-spirited people a way to make **direct contact** without much effort. If someone wanted to insult me fifty years ago, they needed to go to the trouble of writing a letter, buying a stamp, finding out the address of my workplace and sending it. And I probably wouldn't write back. People like that are generally much too lazy to go to that much trouble, but it's different with social media. Now all it takes is a few clicks and they can send whatever sort of message they want.

Social media also means that people can be as **anonymous** as they like. They can make up a **fake** name, put up a **fake** profile picture and tell the most outlandish lies about themselves. They can pretend to be a doctor, a politician, or a world-class jockey, and it's difficult to prove that they're not who they say they are. With that added layer of protection, they feel free to say what they like.

And that's where '**TROLLS**' come from – people who say nasty things on the internet, often looking to get a reaction from the person they're insulting. A 'troll' doesn't have to be anonymous. Sometimes you might know them. They might be someone you've met only a few times or they might be someone in your school, someone in your class, maybe even someone that you used to be friends with.

Trolls come in all shapes and sizes, but they can all be beaten with one simple step:

clicking the  button.

Social media and the internet should be a place where like-minded people come together to communicate and share information about subjects they love.

Someone who uses the internet to upset other people obviously doesn't understand what social media is for, and it's best not to engage with them at all. A quick swipe to delete them as a friend or a follower, or a simple tap of the 'block' button will make sure they don't get any more attention. That means you and I can go back to using social media the way it's meant to be used.

Sometimes people on the internet aren't looking to annoy you or hurt you. Instead, they might say or do something that makes you feel **uncomfortable**, like sending emojis or photos or videos. If what they're sending makes you feel a bit weird or worried, even just for a moment, then it's a good idea to **STOP communicating** with the person and chat to a parent, a guardian or someone else who you trust.

Don't worry, adults sometimes have problems on social media too. Here's a few quick pointers that I tell myself to make sure that I'm using social media safely.

Check your friends or followers list and make sure that they're definitely who they say they are. If you come across a friend or follower that you don't recall meeting before, check if you have any mutual friends and ask your friends who the person is. If you can't remember or find out who they are, it might not be a good idea to let them follow you.

Always think before posting, especially if you're giving information about yourself: your address, private information about friends and family or something personal from your life. Many apps now let you share certain updates with a close circle of friends, not all your followers at once. Making a list of really close friends and allowing nobody but them to see certain posts could be a good idea.

We all sometimes say stupid things online – even adults. Before you post a huge rant about something or someone who's annoying you, just ask yourself: 'How would my granny feel if she saw this?' If the rant is about your granny or your granny's cooking, you have to be extra careful!

Remember, the 'block' button is right there ready to be clicked. If trolls, friends, classmates or random strangers are making you feel bad about yourself, block them and talk to an adult who you trust. Don't bottle up bad feelings.

UNDERSTANDABLE Language

Sometimes people (especially journalists) use big words to make you think that they're smarter than they actually are, even when a perfectly normal word would do the job.

Here are a few examples:

Hippopotomonstrosesquippedaliophobic

Nothing to do with hippos – this is a person with a fear of long words (though I understand hippos generally dislike long words too).

Example: *'When I'm writing news stories, I like to use short and clear language, just in case there are any hippopotomonstrosesquippedaliophobics reading them.'*

Floccinaucinihilipilification

A very long word that just means deciding something is a bit useless.

Example: *'I was reading a book about journalism this morning and had a sudden burst of floccinaucinihilipilification, so I threw the book out the window.'*

Pulchritudinous

You use this word to describe something that's beautiful, which is sort of strange because it's a very ugly-looking word (sorry, 'pulchritudinous').

Example: *'Wow, that really is a **pulchritudinous** sunset.'*

Boondoggle

This means work that you do to make it look like you're busy.

Example: *'I finished my maths exercise, but I didn't want to be given any more so I doodled in my book as a **boondoggle**.'*

Circumlocution

Using lots of words when only a few would do.

Example: *'This journalist needs to stop the **circumlocution** and use words that ordinary people understand.'*

Any good newshound knows that using words like the ones above is a big no-no. What use is a red-hot, jaw-dropping, brain-fizzling news story if **no one** can **understand it**?

Using **clear** words doesn't mean using **short** words! Lots of people understand long words, but including words that most people don't use themselves probably means they won't want to read the story. The less circumlocution the better.

SURPRISE STORY

It's your last breakdancing class before the holidays, and the students and dance instructors have gathered in the main dance studio for a prize-giving ceremony.

Most of the prizes have been awarded – Best Babyfreeze, Best Kip-Up, Best Handglide and lots more. But there's one more award: the Best Attendance Award. Every year a big hamper is given to the pupil who hasn't missed a single dance lesson, and everyone gives them a big round of applause.

This year the prize is awarded to Shania McGhie, an amazing dancer who got a standing ovation for her solo performance at this year's show. She hasn't missed any lessons and she even came in during the Christmas holidays when her mum got the dates mixed up.

Shania is awarded her hamper full of sweets and chocolate, and everyone begins to file out of the studio. On the way there, you notice your friend, Casper, in the corridor. He hasn't been very well this year – there's something up with his bones and he's been using a wheelchair most of the time.

Casper didn't win any awards, and even though he'd managed to do some cool dance moves in his wheelchair, another student won Best Dancer. He missed nearly three months of lessons when he had to go to London for a special surgery. He's back now, and feeling a little better, but he wasn't at a lot of the rehearsals and he didn't take part in the dance show.

Casper doesn't say anything to you, but you can tell that he's feeling a wee bit sad. You think to yourself: 'Is it fair that Shania won a prize and Casper didn't?'

Lots of kids miss out on fun stuff for reasons that they can't control. Maybe someone close to them is sick or passes away. Maybe they themselves are ill, like Casper. Or maybe their parents or guardians don't think that dancing is as important as Shania's parents do. Either way, it's not their fault.

And is it right that we give out prizes and awards for attendance, when some kids are at a disadvantage? Maybe it doesn't matter. After all, it's just a hamper and Shania deserves it.

Sounds like a story to me . . .

OVER TO YOU

The doorbell has just rung, which means
the pizza is here and it's time for me to sign off.

In this book I've let you in on a few industry secrets —
from sniffing out and tracking down a source to writing
your very own news story. There are stories out there
in the wild that will make people laugh and cry. There
are stories that will tell people what they need to
know in order to understand the world around them.
And there are stories out there that will change
people's lives.

A journalist's mission is to find them and tell them.
It sounds simple, but newshounds know that that
couldn't be further from the truth. I hope this book will
help you to find the news that matters to you and to
spot whether there's more to a story than meets the
eye. We're all writing the first draft of history, so it's
time to get scribbling.

But remember to always watch out for FAKE NEWS. It's never been more important to be able to tell the real from the rubbish than it is today. You might still be fooled by Fake News now and again, but what's important is that you try the best you can to keep the world as honest as possible. Because fact is always so much more interesting than fiction.

Memorise the Newshound Commandments, pop this book in your backpack and you can handle any story beamed through a computer or pinged to your phone. Be curious, be fair and be kind. But, most importantly, have fun.

And with that, it's over to you.

WHERE TO NOW?

I can only put so much information into one book. But never fear, the websites and blogs on the next page contain some of the most reliable journalism on the planet! As the headlines keep coming, you can check out these websites to make sure you're getting all the facts.

https://fullfact.org/

Full Fact is an enormous website with a team of brilliant journalists dedicated to debunking myths and Fake News.

https://www.bbc.co.uk/news/reality_check

Chris Morris and his gang of trailblazing reporters create handy videos and blogs that make seemingly complicated stories a lot easier to understand.

https://www.channel4.com/news/factcheck

Like the BBC, Channel 4 also has its own fact-checking service, verifying claims on stories big and small from all around the world.

https://www.thejournal.ie/factcheck/news/

Based in Dublin, Ireland, TheJournal.ie is an excellent resource for finding out the truth about viral stories, controversial quotes and bewildering statistics.

https://apnews.com/hub/ap-fact-check

If you follow global stories, then you should make sure you check out the AP fact-checker. AP is one of the most famous and reliable news outlets in the world and they even have weekly Fake News round-ups: *'A look at what didn't happen this week'*.

A NEWSROOM GLOSSARY

Great reporters and news fans need to be familiar with many words and phrases that journalists use all the time – they're a bit like a code. In my long and distinguished career, I've learned over a thousand words and I can remember at least thirty of them. Here are some you should know:

ANCHOR: The presenter of a news programme – absolutely nothing to do with the heavy metal hooks that keep luxury yachts from floating away or being stolen by gangs of vicious seals.

ANONYMOUS: Someone who wants to be anonymous will give you information as long as you never reveal that they told you. I learned this from an anonymous source: my former English teacher who I can't name here because he's anonymous.

BREAKING NEWS: A piece of news about an event that has literally just happened.

BLOOPER: When a TV presenter or reporter makes a mistake. An example would be forgetting what to say, laughing uncontrollably, or having a huge strawberry jam stain on your tie while reading the news.

CASE STUDY: This is a normal member of the public whose life has been impacted by the story that a journalist is telling. The foundation of almost every report is an interview with a case study, otherwise the article won't show how a story affects real people's lives.

CLICKBAIT: The kind of report produced by online journalists and reporters who write ridiculous and often untrue headlines to make you click on the story. Something like: **'THIS FISH BEARS A REMARKABLE RESEMBLANCE TO THE WORLD'S BIGGEST CELEBRITY'**. That sort of headline is clickbait.

DEADLINE: The time of day when a story needs to be finished, for example when a news programme goes on air or when a newspaper is printed. If a deadline is missed, that means a big gap in the programme or on the page, which will then probably need to be filled by pictures of cute animals, panicked-looking reporters babbling to fill time, or advertisements for second-hand cars.

FOR SALE: 1994 FORD FIESTA, AVERAGE CONDITION 300,000 MILES ON THE CLOCK. SLIGHT ODOUR OF VANILLA MILKSHAKE DUE TO A SUDDEN UNEXPECTED STOP ON BATH STREET IN 2004

EDITOR: The big boss of the newsroom who decides what stories to cover. They usually have a very red face from shouting at everyone.

EXCLUSIVE: A story that a journalist finds and writes about before anyone else. They often come from anonymous sources (thanks again, Mr Pender).

EYEWITNESS: A person who saw something happen with their own eyes. Someone who read about it, or heard about it in a coffee shop, isn't an eyewitness.

FAKE NEWS: A story that isn't true. Also known as a lie.

HARD NEWS: A story that is very serious. Stocks and shares, the price of the pound etc. (N.B. I've never really understood why there's so much discussion about the 'price of the pound'. Surely the clue is in the name? Anyway, I digress).

KICKER: The opposite of 'hard news'. These are stories that will make you feel good about your day. Puppies who have learned sign language, a group of alpacas visiting a nursing home, a baby winning the lottery . . . you get the idea.

MOJO: This term comes from two words squeezed together: 'mobile' and 'journalism'. MoJo is TV and radio reports that have been recorded and edited on a smartphone. Many of the reports you see on the news will actually be filmed on phones, but you might not realise. It's not ideal to film EVERY report on a phone, but they can fit into tiny spaces, be thrown in the air (careful!) and sometimes even go underwater. In those moments, they give you amazing shots that a large camera couldn't.

NEWSHOUND: Someone who is absolutely obsessed with news stories and what's happening in the world around them. Most of the time this means journalists, but if you're reading this book, then it also means you! I don't know why exactly we call these people newshounds. Perhaps a particularly clever Labrador or Catahoula Bulldog established a career in news reporting in the past and the name stuck.

PACKAGE: Another word for a TV news report, usually about two to three minutes long.

PLAGIARISM: This is the biggest no-no for all journalists and reporters: copying somebody else's work, for example a Wikipedia article, and passing it off as your own.

SPIKE: To 'spike' a story is to throw it into the bin and forget it. It's called 'spiking' because newspaper editors used to stick articles they didn't like on to a long metal spike on their desk. Sometimes I think my editor would like to stick me on to a long metal spike on their desk, but thankfully I've so far managed to evade capture.

SCOOP: Like an 'exclusive'. This is a story that only one reporter knows about. Not a story about your journey to work or how you spilled a vanilla milkshake all over a car dashboard in 2004. A 'scoop' is a super interesting story that everyone will want to know about.

STOCK SHOTS: These are the shots that you'll see in many television reports: shots of people's feet walking down the high street, the outside of important buildings like courthouses, and older people in care homes. They're always on hand in TV newsrooms so that you can slot them into reports at short notice. They're sometimes called 'wallpaper', because they provide something nice but not distracting to look at while a reporter tells the audience something important.

VOICEOVER: Sometimes abbreviated to 'VO' – the voice of the reporter that will float over the videos you see on your screen. This is only used in TV newsrooms because, as we know, newspapers and online articles don't talk to you.

VOX POP: A term that means 'voice of the people' and involves a reporter going out and asking ordinary folk their opinion about a particular story.

ABOUT THE AUTHOR

Born at a very young age, Nick Sheridan spent his childhood annoying adults with questions, being curious about the world around him and forcing his parents to watch his one-man performances of Broadway musicals in the front room.

When asked to describe the young Nick, his teachers all have the same response: **'Who?'** Although his time in the classroom may have been unremarkable, his pursuits outside the classroom marked him out as a young man to watch (but not in a suspicious way!).

Nick has reported on all sorts of stories – from a Best Pie Competition to a Muck Obstacle Course (don't ask). And he's reported in all sorts of locations – from a swimming pool full of dogs to up a tree hiding from a swarm of bees.

For two years, Nick worked as a presenter with news2day, a young people's news programme in his native Ireland. During that time he met thousands of children, reported on countless stories and ate enormous amounts of pastries from school bake sales.

He then worked as a Consumer Affairs Correspondent with BBC News and is now a TV and radio presenter based in Glasgow.

In his spare time, he's a keen napper, runner and loser of pens.

BREAKING NEWS:
How to Tell What's REAL from What's RUBBISH
is his first book.

ACKNOWLEDGEMENTS

The world of children's books is a totally new one for me. Thankfully, my agent, Lydia Silver, has been a patient guide through this new and strange landscape, along with Clare Wallace and everyone at the Darley Anderson Children's Book Agency. Thank you for your endless enthusiasm and wisdom over the last year.

To my editor, Amina Youssef, and all the team at Simon & Schuster – thank you for your trust in me as a writer. And thank you to Debbie Foy, Anna Bowles and Leena Lane for bringing the structure and language into sharper focus.

I'm immensely grateful to my family at the BBC for being so generous with their encouragement and advice, much of which has found its way into this book. Thanks to Hayley Valentine, Gary Smith, Gerry Gay, Howard Simpson, Jackie Houston, Annie McGuire, Fraser Wilson and Julie Heekin for their wise words. To the colleagues and friends across the BBC who have kept me buoyant and (somewhat) productive throughout 2020 and 2021 – there are too many of you to name, but thank you.

Thanks to Avril Hoare and Anne-Marie Smyth with RTÉ news2day, for igniting a passion in me for communicating news to young people in an engaging and exciting way.

For countless opportunities and much-needed guidance – thanks to Bob Hughes, Kevin Bakhurst, Hilary McGouran and Denice McNamara.

Thank you to the Wexford writers who I hope have imbued my own writing with that distinct accent: Eoin Colfer, Colm Tóibín, Billy Roche, Mary O'Byrne.

Thank you to Leah Franchetti and Marc Moscardini for giving me an insight into the classroom. And speaking of teachers – thanks to those who encouraged me to write and generally act the eejit in the name of 'creativity', especially to Nick O'Brien, Martin Pender, Eddie Roche and Gerry Haugh.

For their invaluable experience, and their willingness to share it, thank you to Stevie Jackson and Alison Craig.

I also owe an enormous debt to the friends who have faithfully seen me through the last eighteen months: Fiona Stalker, Cat MacKinnon, Laura McGhie, James Atkinson, David Atkinson, Nathan Jackson, Derek McLaughlin, Emma Cameron, Sarah McMullan, Steph Docherty, Franchesca Hashemi, Robbie Armstrong, Roisin Treacy, Sam Griffin, Valerie Loftus, Derek O'Brien, Andrew Lennon, Nicky Ryan, Ciaran O'Connor, Leah Kieran, Isabella Blanchard, Gordon Campbell and many others.

Lil Chris Ward – for being the voice of reason when I'm getting overexcited.

Vanessa Taaffe – my housemate/wife/mother/dance partner and everything in between – thank you.

Brian and Viv, just two of thousands of teachers fighting the good fight every day – keep it up.

And finally to my editors-in-chief, my parents: this book is for you.